Intermittent Fasting For Women Over 50

An easy guide to effectively lose weight, detox, reset metabolism, rejuvenate and increase energy. Eat healthy with 150+ tasty recipes and 2 eating plans

Patty Parsons

The trademarks that are used are without any consent, and the publication of the trademark is without permission or backing by the trademark owner. All trademarks and brands within this book are for clarifying purposes only and are the owned by the owners themselves, not affiliated with this document.

5.2 LUNCH **68**

5.3 DINNER — **105**

5.4 SALADS 145

## 5.5 SMOOTHIES AND BEVERAGES					**169**

5.6 Soups & Stews 188

CHAPTER 6: MEAL PLAN   228

CHAPTER 7: FIRST MONTH OF INTERMITTENT FASTING 237

CHAPTER 8: EXERCISE SUGGESTION FOR WOMEN OVER 50   242

CHAPTER 9: MISTAKES TO AVOID   247

CHAPTER 10: HEALTHY DIET TIPS AND SUGGESTIONS   252

INTRODUCTION

An eating habit in which fasting intervals are interspersed with periods of eating is known as Intermittent Fasting. Following the recommendations, it is not about determining which meals you should have as it is about determining when you should consume them. This means that a diet in the classic sense should not be used to describe this pattern of eating but rather a pattern of eating itself. It is quite popular among individuals who are active in the health and fitness industries. Fasting strategies such as daily sixteen-hour fasts or fasting for twenty-four hours on alternate days every week are common in this context. Every culture and religion in the world has practiced fasting at some point. Ancient hunters did not have access to shops, freezers, or food throughout the year, as we have now. As a result, humans have acquired the capacity to operate for extended periods even when they are not given food. The truth is that eating three to four meals a day on a steady basis is more natural than fasting from time to time. It is also customary in many faiths to practice fasting for religious or spiritual reasons.

It is sometimes referred to as intermittent caloric restriction since it involves restricting when and how much you consume, and on occasion, both. Several approaches may be used to do this. Every other day, you eat the same way you normally do. Alternate-day fasting is the term used to describe this practice. You eat just one meal that supplies 20 percent of your daily calorie needs on the days in between. The majority of individuals use one of the following methods such as alternating between fasting and eating, fasting for a total of sixteen hours every day or fasting for twenty-four hours twice a week on alternate days. There are several techniques to choose from when it comes to intermittent fasting, all of which include splitting the day or week between eating and fasting. It is necessary to eat either very little or no food throughout the day to keep your fasting status intact.

CHAPTER 1: WHAT HAPPENS TO WOMEN'S BODIES AFTER 50?

This chapter gives detail about the effects of aging on women's bodies after 50. How changes take place in the Reproductive system, Nervous system, Endocrine system, cardiovascular system & many more are included in the chapter. Effects of these aging changes with respect to different hormonal variations are also discussed in detail and depth.

1.1 Reproductive System

Menopause is a natural part of the aging process for women. Menopause strikes most women around the age of 50, however, it may strike earlier. The typical age range is about 45-55 years old. Menopause occurs when the ovaries cease producing progesterone & estrogen, and your monthly cycles end. The ovaries cease releasing eggs as well. You cannot become pregnant anymore after menopause.

Overall, certain hormones decline with aging, while others remain constant. Hormones that are often reduced include:

- Renin

- Calcitonin

- Aldosterone

- Growth hormone

Prolactin & Estrogen levels in women are often reduced.

Hormones that usually stay the same or just slightly decrease are:

- Cortisol

- Insulin

- Epinephrine

- Thyroid hormones (T4 & T3)

As men become older, their testosterone levels tend to drop.

Hormones that are likely to rise include:

- (LH) Luteinizing hormone

- Parathyroid hormone

- (FSH) Follicle stimulating hormone

- Norepinephrine

1.3 Immune System

Immune system becomes less effective as you get older. The immune system may alter in the following ways: The immunological system's response time slows down. This raises your chances of being ill. Immunizations such as flu vaccinations or other ones may not function as effectively as they should or shield you for about as long as you anticipate. It's possible, a condition of autoimmune will emerge. This is a condition in which your immunological system basically kills & targets healthy tissues of body by mistake. It's possible that your body may take longer to recover. Healing is more difficult since there are insufficient immunological cells in the body. The capacity of the immune system to identify and cure cell abnormalities deteriorates as well. This may result in a higher cancer risk.

1.4 Nervous System

Your nervous & brain system go through some usual changes as you get older. Weight & nerve cells are lost mostly in spinal cord & brain, also known as atrophy. Your nerve cells may start to send signals more slowly than before. Aging causes a slowing of cognition, memory, and reasoning. These changes do not occur in everyone at the same time. Nerve damage might cause

problems with your senses. You may have lost or had your reflexes or sensations diminished. This causes issues with mobility & safety.

1.5 Cardiovascular System

The heart normally keeps pumping sufficient blood to nourish all of the body's organs. When you make an older heart work harder, that might unable to pump blood properly. The following are some of the factors that affect the heart to work harder:

- Emotional stress

- Some particular medicines

- Physical exertion

- Infections

- Illness

- Injuries

The following are some examples of blood vessels & heart issues:

- Deep-vein-thrombosis

- Blood clots

- Thrombophlebitis

- Varicose veins

- Peripheral-vascular-disease

- Aneurysms

1.6 Muscular and Skeletal System

Men & women's bone density starts to deteriorate around the age of 30. After menopause, women's bone density loss increases. As a consequence, bones become increasingly weak and prone to breaking, particularly as people age. Changes in connective tissue & cartilage influence people's joints as they age. Sarcopenia is a progressive loss of muscle that begins around the age of 30 and continues throughout life. Aging has an impact on the different kinds of muscle tissues.

1.7 HGH production

Several catabolic consequences accompany normal aging, including a loss of lean mass, an increase in your fat mass, and a loss in bone density. A clinical picture known as somatopause is associated with certain physiologic changes: frailty, relative obesity, muscular atrophy, increased fracture frequency, and sleep disturbances. Without a doubt, these clinical indications of aging are the result of a complicated collection of alterations that include, at least to some extent, the (GH) Growth Hormone-axis.

And in comparison to the popular belief that GH shortage causes aging, evidence suggests that high or even normal levels of Growth hormone may hasten the aging process.

Other effects of Aging include:

- Cataracts & refractive errors.

- Hearing loss

- Osteoarthritis

- Depression & dementia

- Diabetes etc

CHAPTER 2: INTERMITTENT FASTING FOR WOMEN OVER 50

This chapter gives detail about the Intermittent fasting. How does it work, is it safe and when not to follow IF are included in the chapter. Benefits, as well as risks of IF for women over 50, are also discussed in detail and depth.

2.1 What is Intermittent Fasting?

An eating habit in which fasting intervals are interspersed with periods of eating is known as intermittent fasting. Following the recommendations, it is not about determining which meals you should have as it is about determining when you should consume them. This means that a diet in the classic sense should not be used to describe this pattern of eating but rather a pattern of eating itself.

2.2 How does Intermittent Fasting work?

IF can be done through multiple methods, but they are all revolve on selecting regular fasting & eating times. For example, you may try eating just for eight hours a day and fasting for the rest of the day. Alternatively, you might opt to eat just one meal each day, 2 days per week. There are multiple methods of intermittent fasting regimens to choose from.

2.3 Is Intermittent fasting safe?

The most common negative effect of IF is hunger. You also may feel tired, and your mind may not function as effectively as it once did. This will only be momentary since your body will need time to adjust to the new food plan. Before attempting intermittent fasting, ask your doctor if you've any medical issues.

All things considered, IF has an excellent safety record. If you're well-nourished & healthy throughout, going without food for a period isn't risky.

Benefits of Intermittent fasting for women over 50 include the following:

- Balanced blood sugar levels

- Better cardiovascular health

- Better sex drive

- Blood pressure and cholesterol

- Cellular repair

- Easy to follow

- Effect on circadian rhythm

- Energy levels

- Heart health

- HGH

- Increased growth hormone

- Longevity

- Lose weight and visceral fat

- Oxidative damage

- Polycystic ovarian syndrome

- Reduced risk of Alzheimer's and better cognitive health

- Reduces the risk of cancer

- Regulating inflammation

- Skin health

- Weight loss maintenance

Risks of Intermittent fasting for women over 50 include the following:

- Dehydration

- Extreme Hunger

- Malnutrition

- Mood swings

- Overeating and Binge eating

- Stress Hormone

- Tiredness

2.4 When women should not fast?

IF may not be quite as advantageous for females as it is beneficial for males, according to some data. Women's menstrual periods halted when they began performing IF and returned to usual when they restarted their old eating pattern, according to anecdotal evidence. Consider delaying intermittent fasting for the time being if you do have reproductive concerns or are attempting to conceive. If you're breast-feeding or pregnant, this pattern of eating is probably not a good option.

Chapter 3: The right type of intermittent

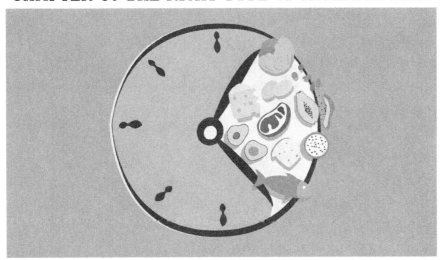

This chapter gives detail about the types of Intermittent fasting. How do each and every single type works is discussed in detail and depth.

▰▰▰ 3.1 16:8 Method

You should restrict your eating to an 8-hour window with two-three meals and then fast for sixteen hours during that period. Consume food until 6 pm after dinner, then postpone breakfast until 10 am the next day, consume food for eight hours, and the cycle begins all over again the following day. If necessary, you may change the time to meet your requirements; for example, depending on your schedule, you may choose to eat earlier or later in the day.

3.2 14:10 Method

You can fast for about 14 hours and then eat within a window of 10-hour if you practice 14:10 type of intermittent fasting. You'll miss breakfast if you fast at 14:10 am or early time of fasting, and supper if you fast at 14:10 pm or late time of fasting. Every day, you should eat around 1400 to 1600 kcal.

3.3 12:12 Method

One of the IF approaches is the 12:12 rule, which states that instead of eating whenever you want, you must consume your daily calorie intake within twelve hours and then go with no food for the upcoming 12 hrs. The body will transform its fat reserves into energy with the passing time as a result of the daily 12-hr fasting window, generating ketones in the circulation of blood.

3.4 20:4 Method

It is a time-restricted eating pattern that consists of a twenty-hour fast followed by a four-hour feeding window. In general, you may eat to your heart's content during the four-hour feasting period, but it is difficult to consume an excessive amount of calories in such a short period by default. However, you may observe it at any time of day that is suitable for you. The 4-hour eating window is often observed in the evening, but

you may observe it at any time of day that is convenient for you. Two meals are permitted between 3 pm and 7 pm, followed by a twenty-hour fast the next day after that.

3.5 5:2 Method

To follow this diet, you should eat what you typically eat five days a week and restrict your calorie intake to 600 calories on the other two days of the week. This diet, often known as the fast diet, is quite restrictive. According to the guidelines, females should have 500 calories, and males should consume 600 calories on fasting days. This diet is effective in terms of lowering the proportion of body fat carried by the individual. Calories might be ingested in multiple little meals throughout the day or in a single large meal at one time. During the last five days of the fast, there are no restrictions on what you may eat.

3.6 Eat Stop Eat

Depending on your schedule, a twenty-four-hour fast is observed once or twice a week under the Eat and Stop approach. Over the previous several decades, this method has achieved universal recognition. It is similar to fasting for a full twenty-four-hour period if you go from dinner one day to dinner the next day. Example: If you finish dinner at 8 pm one day and don't eat again until dinner at 8 pm the next day, you will have successfully finished a twenty-four-hour fast. You may also fast

from one meal to another, for example, from breakfast to breakfast or lunch to lunch, and the result will be the same as fasting from one meal to another. Solid meals are not authorized; however, liquids such as water and coffee are tolerated in limited quantities.

3.7 Alternate Day Fasting

As the name indicates, this regimen includes fasting every other day, part of the process. On fasting days, eating is restricted to a single 500-calorie meal or complete fasting, depending on the occasion, without any calories being consumed in between. The days in between may be spent eating normally; nevertheless, as with any fasting period, ketosis is recommended throughout this period. In the long term, this is a difficult sort of fasting that is unlikely to be continued. This approach is available in several different configurations.

3.8 Spontaneous Meal Skipping

Most of the advantages of IF intermittent fasting may be obtained without following a planned strategy. Another alternative is to skip meals on sometimes, e.g., when you aren't hungry or when you are too preoccupied to prepare your meals and then eat. Some individuals, on the other hand, eat after few hours to avoid going into starvation state or losing muscle.

While others' bodies are built to withstand extended periods of fasting and can go without 1 or 2 meals on occasion. You are the only one who really understands yourself.

A spontaneous IF is basically when you skip 1 or 2 meals whenever you feel like it. During the eating hours, just be sure you consume nutritious and balanced meals.

3.9 The Warrior Diet

During a day, you consume little portions of raw veggies &

fruits, and at night, you eat one large meal. Mainly, you fast throughout the day and eat inside a eating window of 4 hrs at night. One of the earliest popular diets that involved a sort of IF intermittent fasting was the Warrior Diet. The food options on this diet are very identical to those on the paleo-diet, consisting largely of pure, unprocessed foods.

3.10 Crescendo Fasting

The name crescendo fasting accurately captures its goal, progressively increasing the quantity of fasting your body can tolerate easily. So, for instance, you may fast for about 14 hours, beginning at 9 p.m. on Sunday and ending at 11 a.m. on Monday. After that, you'll eat regularly for the following few days before repeating the fast in a same manner.

CHAPTER 4: LET'S BEGIN!

This chapter gives detail about how to start Intermittent fasting step by step. Which things to keep in mind when doing IF and how you can achieve your desired goals efficiently are all discussed in detail and depth.

4.1 How Do You Start Your Intermittent Fasting?

Some healthy tips and tricks to make your IF efficient are as follows:

Some dietary requirements with age

While practicing IF, you should take suitable dietary intakes (enough nutrients and calories) with respect to appropriate age.

Start by making a list of your goals

Follow schedule of your required achievements and move step by step from easy to intense practice during IF.

Short-term goals matter

By working on short-term goals consistently, you can efficiently achieve long term goals.

Gather the tools

Prepare your meals in advance so that you can easily enjoy appropriate food during busy routine.

Start slow

Manage your eating and fasting patterns slowly. There is no need to opt a drastic change.

Carrot and stick approach

Use Carrot and stick approach to improve your motivation; that is how you can follow proper meals during eating patterns.

Deal with hunger pangs

Learn how to deal with hunger pangs during the fasting period, and then arrange your meals accordingly.

Know what to eat and practice portion control

Learn what you should eat and what to avoid while following IF, and how to eat in little portions after a specific duration of fasting.

Be patient

Have patience for the results because when you start something new and challenging simultaneously, it takes time to adjust to it, and one can achieve gradual progress.

Reward yourself

Try to motivate yourself with little rewards, e.g., have your favorite snack during the eating period after fasting.

Create accountability

Plan accountability after a few days to check whether you are taking the right meals or not, following the right patterns of fasting or not.

Concentrate on the positive

Try to practice overall good health. Focus on the progress instead of perfectionism.

Breaking your fast

If you start to feel problematic hunger during fasting periods, get a break from fasting right that time.

Dirty fast vs clean fast

When you fast clean, you only intake water or calorie-free liquids like mineral water, tap water, sparkling water, black tea & black coffee. You may come across knowledge that states that clean fasting has to be calorie-free. Still, liquids such as Black

coffee, on the other hand, has 5 calories/cup. Those few calories, therefore, are insignificant.

When you ingest foods or liquids with less than 50 calories within your fasting periods, this is known as dirty fasting. If you drink delicious bone broth or add a little cream to your cup of coffee, you're following dirty fast. Alternatively, you might sweeten your tea with calorie-free sweeteners or consume soda with 0 calorie.

Both methods of fasting are acceptable depending upon your objectives. In the end, you should go with whichever method best fits for you, whether it's via trial & error, objectives or progress, personal preference.

The mindset is everything

The charm of IF intermittent fasting is that there is no right way or wrong way to do it. It's just a tool you can use to enhance your wellness in whichever manner works best for you. Hence, your mindset is everything that makes you to motivate for doing the right things.

Supplements

Try to take proper and enough nutritional supplements required according to your body's dietary needs.

Protein

Consume foods rich in protein to gain enough energy during eating periods and plan your meals accordingly.

CHAPTER 5: RECIPES FOR INTERMITTENT FASTING

This chapter will help you to learn and experiment with the different basic varieties of recipes that are used on a daily basis in the breakfast, lunch, dinner timing as well as for smoothies & beverages, soups & stews, salads & desserts regarding an Intermittent fasting diet. It definitely consists of an infinite number of options to try according to your flavor, with nutritional information for each given recipe.

5.1 Breakfast

BAKED AVOCADO & EGGS WITH CHEDDAR CHIVES

Prep time: 5mins   **Cook time: 5mins**

Servings: 4

Nutritional information:

Per serving: Kcal 179, Fat: 12g, Carbs: 12g, Protein: 5g

Ingredients

→ 50g cheddar cheese grated

→ 1 mashed avocado

→ 2 flour wraps tortilla

Direction

On one tortilla wraps, spread half cheese. Spread mashed avocado over the borders. The leftover cheese should be sprinkled on top, following the second one. Over moderate flame, heat a frying pan. Place quesadilla carefully inside the pan, then cook for 2 to 3 minutes. Gently turn the quesadilla with a spatula, then cook for another 2-3 minutes. Serve immediately after slicing.

Avocado Salad with Shrimp/Prawn and Cajun Potato

Prep time: 5mins   **Cook time: 15mins**

Servings: 2

Nutritional information:

Per serving: Kcal 435, Fat: 23g, Carbs: 37g, Protein: 23g

<table>
<tr><td rowspan="5">Ingredients</td><td>

→ 1 tbsp. of olive oil

→ 300 g potatoes

→ 250 g cooked king prawns

→ 2 sliced spring onions

→ Salt

</td><td>

→ 1 minced garlic clove

→ 1 peeled avocado

→ 2 tsp. of Cajun seasoning

→ 1 cup of alfalfa sprout

</td></tr>
</table>

Direction	Cook potatoes for 10-15 minutes, until cooked, in a saucepan of slightly boiling salted water. Drain thoroughly. Inside a wok or big nonstick skillet, heat some oil. Stir in your prawns, spring onions, garlic, and Cajun spice till the prawns are heated, about 2-3 minutes. Cook for another minute after adding the potatoes. Return to serving plates and garnish with avocado & alfalfa sprouts before serving.

Baked Avocado & Eggs with Cheddar Chives

Prep time: 10mins　　　　**Cook time: 20mins**

Servings: 4

Nutritional information:

Per serving: Kcal 247, Fat: 19g, Carbs: 11g, Protein: 9g

Ingredients	
→ 4 eggs	→ ¼ cup of bacon bits
→ 2 tbsp. of chopped chives	→ pepper
→ 2 avocados	→ cheddar cheese, shredded
→ 1 quartered cherry tomato	→ 1 chopped sprig basil
→ salt	

Direction

Cook potatoes for 10-15 minutes, until cooked, in a saucepan of slightly boiling salted water. Drain thoroughly. Inside a wok or big nonstick skillet, heat some oil. Stir in your prawns, spring onions, garlic, and Cajun spice till the prawns are heated, about 2-3 minutes. Cook for another minute after adding the potatoes. Return to serving plates and garnish with avocado & alfalfa sprouts before serving.

BERRIES WITH BUTTERNUT BREAKFAST

Prep time: 10mins   **Cook time: 1hr 10mins**

Servings: 5

Nutritional information:

Per serving: Kcal 379, Fat: 9g, Carbs: 71g, Protein: 9g

Ingredients	
→ 1 ½ cups of wheat berries red winter	→ 2 tbsp. of olive oil, extra-virgin
→ 3 cups of water	→ 1 tbsp. of maple syrup
→ 2 cups of butternut squash	→ ½ cup of fresh parsley chopped
→ ¼ cup of sliced almonds	→ 1 orange
→ 3 tbsp. of orange juice	→ ¾ cup of dried cranberries

Direction

In a pan, boil the water and include wheat berries. Lower the heat, then cover, and simmer for 45-50 minutes, or until soft. Drain. Bake at 400 °F. Place squash onto a baking tray and mix

with 1 tbsp oil. Roast for 20-30 minutes in already heated oven till tender. Allow squash to chill on a paper towel-lined dish to absorb excess oil. In a mixing bowl, combine orange juice, maple syrup, remaining oil, and orange zest for vinaigrette. I n a bowl, mix prepared wheat berries, vinaigrette, roasted squash, parsley, & cranberries. Allow 10-20 minutes inside the refrigerator to chill. Serve the salad with chopped almonds on upper side.

BERRY PARFAIT

Prep time: 5mins   **Cook time: 0mins**

Servings: 4

Nutritional information:

Per serving: Kcal 313, Fat: 12g, Carbs: 38g, Protein: 14g

Ingredients

→ Granola

→ 1-quart plain yogurt

→ 2-3 cups berries such as strawberries, blueberries, blackberries, raspberries

Direction

Wash then dry your berries; if used, hull & cut the berries into chunks. Fill 4 separate glass bowls/parfait glasses with a layer

of yoghurt. Place a coating of berries on top, followed by a coating of granola. Based on the length of your glass or bowl, repeat the stacking process one or twice more, finishing with a coating of granola.

Black Bean Burrito and Sweet Potato

Prep time: 10mins   Cook time: 30mins

Servings: 3

Nutritional information:

Per serving: Kcal 547, Fat: 12g, Carbs: 16g, Protein: 96g

Ingredients	
→ olive oil	→ guacamole
→ 2 peeled sweet potatoes	→ 1 tsp. of chili powder
→ ½ tsp. of smoked paprika	→ cayenne pepper
→ kosher salt	→ ¾ cup of corn
→ ½ tsp. of garlic powder	→ 15 oz of black beans
→ pepper	→ 3 flour tortillas
→ 1 diced jalapeño	→ diced tomato
→ ½ diced yellow onion	→ chopped lettuce
→ 1 minced clove garlic,	→ vegan cheddar cheese shredded
→ ½ tsp. of ground cumin	

Preheat your oven to 400 degrees Fahrenheit. Toss your sweet potatoes using a spray of olive oil, garlic powder, paprika, salt, & pepper on a baking tray. Toss until everything is evenly covered. Bake approximately 20 minutes, till sweet potato is cooked, turning halfway along. In a saucepan, warm a splash of olive oil on medium heat. Put the onion & sauté for 3 to 4 minutes, till semi-translucent, till the oil starts to shimmer. Sauté for 2 to 3 minutes, or till jalapeno, garlic, cumin, chili powder, & cayenne pepper are aromatic. Add salt ^ pepper, then add lack beans & corn and simmer for 3-4 minutes more, until either warmed throughout. To make a burrito, fill a tortilla with 1\3 of the bean & corn combination 1\3 of the cooked sweet potatoes, tomatoes, lettuce, guacamole and vegan cheese. Fold inside the edges and wrap the pastry, tucking the contents within. Rep with the rest of the ingredients. Serve by slicing in half.

BLUEBERRY NUT OATMEAL

Prep time: 10mins   **Cook time: 23mins**

Servings: 4

Nutritional information:

Per serving: Kcal 179, Fat: 21g, Carbs: 11g, Protein: 13g

Ingredients		
→ 4 cups of water	→ 1/2 cup of blueberries
→ 1 cinnamon	→ 1/4 cup of chopped toasted walnuts
→ 1 cup of Irish steel cut oats	

Direction

Boil some water. Stir in the oats and cook for thirty min, as per the package guidelines. Transfer the oats to dishes and top with blueberries, walnuts, and cinnamon right away.

Bread Pudding with Rhubarb

Prep time: 15mins   **Cook time: 50mins**

Servings: 6

Nutritional information:

Per serving: Kcal 444, Fat: 16g, Carbs: 64g, Protein: 10g

Ingredients	
→ 1 ½ cups of milk	→ 1 ¼ cups of white sugar
→ 8 slices of bread	→ 5 eggs
→ ¼ cup margarine or butter	→ ½ tsp. of ground cinnamon
→ ¼ cup chopped walnuts	→ 2 cups of rhubarb diced
	→ ¼ tsp. of salt

Direction

Preheat oven to 325°F . Bread cubes should be placed in a greased 2-quart baking dish. In a pan, mix the butter and milk and heat until barely boiling. Allow fifteen minutes for the sauce

to soak into the bread cubes. Mix together the sugar, eggs, cinnamon, & salt in a bowl. Add the rhubarb and mix well. Pour over moistened bread, then gently whisk until everything is well combined. Over the surface, put walnuts. In an oven that is already heated, bake about 50 minutes, or till well browned on top. Allow for a ten-minute rest period before serving.

BREAKFAST BUTTERNUT HOT SOUP

Prep time: 20mins   **Cook time: 40mins**

Servings: 4

Nutritional information:

Per serving: Kcal 292, Fat: 15g, Carbs: 28g, Protein: 10g

Ingredients	
→ 8 sage leaves	→ 3 cups of chicken broth
→ ½ pound of breakfast sausage	→ ¼ cup of sherry
→ 1 pound of butternut squash	→ 1 cup of beef broth
→ 2 small chopped carrots,	→ ¼ tsp. of pumpkin pie spice
→ 2 stalks chopped celery,	→ 2 tsp. of brown sugar
→ 4 tsp. of sour cream	→ Ground black pepper
→ 1 small chopped onion,	→ ¼ cup of half-and-half

Direction

5-8 minutes on moderate flame, cook and toss pork sausage inside a big heavy pot/Dutch oven till browned and golden. With a wooden spoon, remove your sausage, keeping the drippings inside the saucepan. Remove the leaves of sage and put them aside after browning them in hot drippings for approximately 30 seconds. In the leftover sausage drippings, heat celery, butternut squash, onion and carrots until cooked, turning just once after approximately 5 minutes. Put in some sherry and whisk to melt any browned pieces of food stuck to pan bottom. Stir in the brown sugar & pumpkin pie spice after adding the beef and chicken broth. Raise the broth to one boil, then lower to a slow heat and cook for twenty minutes, just till the squash is soft. Using an electric mixer, puree the soup, keeping a several vegetable lumps. Add half-and-half & black pepper to taste. Serve the soup in 4 big bowls, adding 1 tsp sour cream, two fried leaves of sage and cooked sausage on top of each dish.

BREAKFAST SHAKE WITH BERRIES

Prep time: 5mins   **Cook time: 5mins**

Servings: 4

Nutritional information:

Per serving: Kcal 125, Fat: 2g, Carbs: 23g, Protein: 6g

Ingredients	
→ 2 cups of berries frozen mixed → 1 ½ cups of almond milk unsweetened → 1 cup of spinach → 1 frozen banana	→ 1 tsp. of honey → ½ tsp of vanilla extract → 2 tsp. of vanilla protein powder

Direction

Inside the jar of the high-powered mixer (Vitamix), combine all the ingredients in specific order. Begin blending on low, then gradually increase to high. Mix for 30 to 60 seconds over high speed, or till smoothie is smooth and lump-free. Immediately pour in glasses & serve.

DIVINE APPLES

Prep time: 15mins   **Cook time: 0mins**

Servings: 4

Nutritional information:

Per serving: Kcal 209, Fat: 7g, Carbs: 29g, Protein: 8g

Ingredients	
→ 1 cup of oats	→ 1 cup of low-fat milk
→ 1 peeled apple	→ ½ tsp. of mixed spice
→ ¼ cup of toasted slivered almonds	→ 1 tbsp. of honey
→ ½ tsp. of ground cinnamon	

Direction

In a big microwave-safe dish, combine the apple, cinnamon, oats, mixed spice, two glasses of water and milk. Cook till 8 mins on high, turning every minute, till thick. Allow 5 minutes to pass. Serve extra honey & slivered almonds sprinkled on top.

EGG PLANT IN SLOW COOKER

Prep time: 15mins   **Cook time: 5mins**

Servings: 4

Nutritional information:

Per serving: Kcal 341, Fat: 12g, Carbs: 51g, Protein: 13g

Ingredients

→ 1 pound of peeled eggplant

→ 1 tbsp. of olive oil

→ 1 large chopped and seeded red bell pepper

→ 4 pieces of pita bread whole wheat

→ 4 diced plum tomatoes

→ 1 large diced and peeled onion

→ 4 minced and peeled cloves garlic

→ 1 large chopped zucchini,

→ 2 tsp. of dried basil

→ 4 ounces of feta cheese vegan

→ salt and pepper

Direction

Put olive into a six-quart crockpot. Combine the bell pepper, eggplant, tomato, garlic, zucchini, salt, dried basil, and pepper inside a large mixing bowl. To be covered with olive oil, mix all the ingredients thoroughly. Cook on slow for five hours or maximum for three hours with the cover on the slow cooker. Toss in the feta cheese crumbles. It's time to eat.

Eggs & Bacon with Pecans & Coconut

Prep time: 15mins   **Cook time: 45mins**

Servings: 9

Nutritional information:

Per serving: Kcal 668, Fat: 56g, Carbs: 34g, Protein: 15g

Ingredients

→ 2 cups of coconut chips unsweetened

→ 8 slices of thick-cut bacon

→ ½ cup of ground flaxseed

→ 1 cup of sunflower seeds

→ 1 cup of rolled oats

→ ½ cup of sliced pitted dates

→ ½ cup of pecans chopped

→ ½ cup of sliced almonds

→ ½ cup of hazelnuts chopped

→ ⅓ cup of canola or coconut oil

→ ½ tsp. of cinnamon

→ ⅓ cup of maple syrup

→ 1 egg white

→ ¼ tsp. of kosher salt

Direction

Preheat the oven to 325°F. Cook the bacon until it is cooked through but not crisp, then slice it into tiny pieces. Combine the bacon, flaxseed, coconut chips, oats, nuts and sunflower seeds in a large mixing bowl. Heat the syrup, oil, cinnamon, & salt in a pot. Combine the nut combination and pour over it. Spread granola on your baking sheet after mixing in egg white. Bake for 20-25 minutes, or till somewhat dried out, and cool for twenty minutes on the pan. Add the dates and mix well. Refrigerate for up to five days if stored in a sealed jar.

FRITTATA DI POLENTA

Prep time: 15mins   **Cook time: 30mins**

Servings: 5

Nutritional information:

Per serving: Kcal 170, Fat: 21g, Carbs: 22g, Protein: 21g

Ingredients	
→ 4 medium eggs	→ 10 g of Parmesan cheese
→ 400 g Frozen peas	→ 100 g of Red onion
→ Salt & Pepper	→ 2 g of Thyme picked
→ 125 g of Ricotta cheese	→ 5 ml of Olive oil

Direction

In a heated oven proof skillet/frying pan with a 20m in diameter and a finely sliced onion, sweat your onions till soft and transparent. Cook till the frozen and defrosted peas, then remove from the heat and leave aside it to cool. Meanwhile, whisk together the grated parmesan, eggs, and spices in a mixing dish. Put 1/2 of egg mixture to peas & onions that have been evenly distributed. Dollop your ricotta evenly using a tsp, pour the remaining egg mixture over top. Preheat oven to 180°C and bake for 30 mins.

FAST BANANA BERRIES BREAKFAST

Prep time: 5mins   **Cook time: 0mins**

Servings: 1

Nutritional information:

Per serving: Kcal 433, Fat: 17g, Carbs: 64g, Protein: 12g

Ingredients

→ 3-4 sliced medium strawberries

→ ½ sliced banana

→ ½ cup of nondairy milk

→ ¼ cup of blueberries

→ ½ cup of raw old-fashioned oats gluten free

→ ⅛ cup of chopped raw walnuts

→ 1 tbsp. of flax meal optional

→ 1-2 teaspoon of cinnamon

Direction

In a small mixing basin, combine all of the dry ingredients, then stir thoroughly. Over the dry ingredients, add non-dairy milk. Eat.

Mum's Supper Club le Parmesan

Prep time: 25mins   **Cook time: 35mins**

Servings: 10

Nutritional information:

Per serving: Kcal 487, Fat: 16g, Carbs: 62g, Protein: 24g

Ingredients

→ 2 beaten eggs

→ 3 sliced and peeled eggplant

→ 6 cups of spaghetti sauce

→ ½ tsp. of dried basil

→ 4 cups of bread crumbs Italian seasoned

→ ½ cup of Parmesan cheese, grated divided

→ 1 shredded package mozzarella cheese

Direction

Preheat the oven to 350°F. After dipping the eggplant pieces in egg, coat them with bread crumbs. Put on a sheet pan in a thin layer. Cook for five mins on every side in a pre-heated oven. Line the bottom of baking dish with spaghetti sauce. Inside the sauce, arrange a eggplant layer slices. Cheeses of mozzarella & parmesan are sprinkled on top. Finish with some cheeses before continuing with the other ingredients. Garnish with basil. Cook for 35 mins, or till golden brown, inside a pre-heated oven.

HOT CEREAL WITH MIXED GRAINS

Prep time: 5mins   **Cook time: 30mins**

Servings: 4

Nutritional information:

Per serving: Kcal 169, Fat: 11g, Carbs: 24g, Protein: 32g

Ingredients

→ ¼ cup of date paste or 4 Medjool dates	→ 1-2 Tbsp of chia seeds or ground flax
→ 4 cups of plant-based milk	→ 1 cup of steel cut oats
→ 1 tsp of cinnamon	→ 1 tsp of vanilla extract
→ ½ tsp of ground cloves	→ ½ cup of amaranth
→ ½ tsp of cardamom	→ ½ cup of quinoa
→ ½ tsp of nutmeg	→ Berries (fresh or frozen)

Direction

In a mixer, combine plant-based milk and dates and date paste till smooth. Mix the milk mixture, which is plant-based and spices, in a pot. Bring to boil, then whisk in grains & cover. Cook about thirty min on moderate flame. Fresh or frozen berries may be added on the top.

FRUITY BREAKFAST SALA

Prep time: 15mins   **Cook time: 0mins**

Servings: 6

Nutritional information:

Per serving: Kcal 119, Fat: 1g, Carbs: 29g, Protein: 2g

Ingredients	→ 2 chopped red apples	→ 1 cup red/green grapes
	→ 1 tbsp. of concentrate orange juice	→ 1/2 cup of lemon yogurt
		→ 1 sliced firm banana,
	→ 2 cups of cubed cantaloupe	

Direction

Combine all fruit in a dish. Drizzle on the fruit a mixture of yoghurt & orange juice extract.

OATMEAL WITH PECANS & COCONUT

Prep time: 10mins   **Cook time: 0mins**

Servings: 1

Nutritional information:

Per serving: Kcal 327, Fat: 14g, Carbs: 45g, Protein: 10g

Ingredients	
→ 1 tbsp. of shredded coconut unsweetened	→ ⅛ tsp. of ground cinnamon
→ ⅓ cup of steel cut oats	→ ½ tsp. of brown sugar
→ 1 tbsp. of milk	→ ⅓ cup of milk
→ 1 tbsp. of crushed pecans	

Direction

In a container, combine the oats, pecans, coconut, cinnamon and brown sugar; top over with 1/3 cup of milk. Chill for eight hours or night, covered. Before serving, add 1 tbsp milk to the oat mixture.

OMELET WITH CHEDDAR CITRU & MUSHROOMS

Prep time: 5mins   **Cook time: 10mins**

Servings: 2

Nutritional information:

Per serving: Kcal 294, Fat: 18g, Carbs: 14g, Protein: 19g

Ingredients

→ Salt

→ 3 eggs

→ Snipped chives

→ 2 tsp. of and 1 tsp. of unsalted butter

→ 4 ounces crimini mushrooms

→ 1/2 onion

→ 2 tbsp. of shredded cheddar

Direction

In a dish, beat the eggs & add a touch of salt. Set aside after whisking until fully combined. In a 10-inch heavy nonstick pan placed over moderate flame, melt 2 tablespoons butter. Add onions, then cook for 3-5 minutes, or until tender and transparent. Add mushrooms, then cook for another 3 minutes, or till they lose their juices, then become soft. Put aside the onions & mushrooms in a mixing dish. Wipe the skillet out and pour in 1 tsp oil or butter to cover the pan. Pour beaten eggs into the pan. When the sides of the omelet start to firm, slide a silicon/rubber scraper around the perimeter, gently pushing the edge away and rotating the pan to allow any raw egg to flow beneath the omelet. Top 1 side of the omelet with the saved sautéed mushrooms & onions whenever the egg surface is nearly set. If using, put cheese over top evenly. Carefully flip the opposite side of the omelet onto the filling using a spatula. Cook for yet another minute, till the cheese, melts as well as the egg is done, on the opposite side of the packed omelet. Put to a platter and top with chives that have been freshly cut, if preferred. Serve right away.

OVERNIGHT OATMEAL

Prep time: 5mins   **Cook time: 0mins**

Servings: 1

Nutritional information:

Per serving: Kcal 378, Fat: 11g, Carbs: 54g, Protein: 17g

Ingredients

→ 1/3-1/2 cup of rolled oats old-fashioned

→ 1/3-1/2 cup of liquid like almond, dairy milk, coconut milk or cashew

→ 1/3-1/2 cup of yogurt

→ 1/2 mashed banana

→ 1 tsp. of chia seeds

→ fruit such as nuts, seeds, nut butter, protein powder, coconut, granola, spices, vanilla extract and citrus zest

Direction

In a container or jar, combine the necessary quantities of milk, yoghurt, oats, chia seeds, & banana and mix well. Refrigerate for about at least five hours or full night. If necessary, add more fluids in morning. Garnish with nuts, fruit, seeds, nut butter, granola, protein powder, coconut, zest, spices, or vanilla essence after you've achieved the appropriate consistency.

Pancakes with Blueberry & Almond

Prep time: 20mins   **Cook time: 3mins**

Servings: 6

Nutritional information:

Per serving: Kcal 263, Fat: 12g, Carbs: 30g, Protein: 6g

Ingredients

→ 1 ¼ cups of all-purpose flour

→ 5 tbsp. of butter

→ 2 tbsp. of white sugar

→ 1 cup of fresh blueberries

→ ½ tsp. of salt

→ 1 tbsp. of baking powder

→ 1 cup of plain yogurt

→ 1 ½ tsp. of almond extract

→ 2 eggs

→ ¼ cup of water

Direction

In your microwave-safe bowl, heat 3 tbsp of butter for 20-30 seconds in the microwave. In a large mixing basin, combine the flour, baking powder, sugar, and salt. In a mixing dish, combine the yoghurt plus eggs; stir in the almond essence and melted butter. Using a spatula, fold the flour mix into the yoghurt mixture till well incorporated. 1 tbsp at one time, add a little water until the batter is pourable. Inside a large sized griddle or skillet, melt the remaining butter on moderate flame. Pour ¼ cup of batter into pan and top with 6-10 blueberries; heat for 1-2 minutes, or until batter begins to bubble. Cook for another 30 seconds on the other side, or until the bottom is gently browned. Rep with the rest of the batter & blueberries.

Poached Eggs & Avocado Toast

Prep time: 5mins   **Cook time: 5mins**

Servings: 1

Nutritional information:

Per serving: Kcal 393, Fat: 20g, Carbs: 30g, Protein: 23g

Ingredients		
→ 2 eggs	→ Salt & pepper
→ 2 slices of grain bread whole	→ Fresh herbs (thyme, parsley, or basil)
→ 1/3 avocado	→ Heirloom tomatoes
→ 2 tbsp. of Parmesan cheese shaved	

Direction

To begin, bring a saucepan of water to a boil. Place the rim made of metal of 2 mason jar tops in pot, firmly just on bottom. Turn the heat down once the water boils and delicately break the eggs through each rim. Top the saucepan with a lid and cook for 5mins. Toast your bread and crush the avocado on every slice of toast whilst eggs continue cooking. Whenever the eggs become ready, take them out from water with a spatula. Put the cooked eggs on the bread, then gently remove the rims off eggs. Serve alongside fresh cut into quarters heirloom tomatoes and a sprinkle of Parmesan cheese, fresh herbs and salt.

Pudding with Corn

Prep time: 10mins   **Cook time: 1hour**

Servings: 8

Nutritional information:

Per serving: Kcal 277, Fat: 12g, Carbs: 39g, Protein: 7g

Ingredients

- → ⅓ cup of butter, melted
- → 2 cans of cream-style corn
- → 5 eggs
- → ¼ cup of white sugar
- → 4 tbsp. of cornstarch
- → ½ cup of milk
- → 1 can of corn kernels

Direction

Preheat the oven 400°F. Oil a 2-quart baking dish with cooking spray. Thoroughly beat eggs inside a large mixing basin.

Combine the sugar, melted butter, & milk in a mixing bowl. In a separate bowl, whisk together the cornstarch and the water. Combine the corn & creamed corn in a mixing bowl. Blend it well. Pour the ingredients into the casserole dish that has been prepared. 1 hour in the oven

Breakfast Quinoa Pudding

Prep time: 5mins   **Cook time: 35mins**

Servings: 6

Nutritional information:

Per serving: Kcal 202, Fat: 1g, Carbs: 42g, Protein: 4g

Ingredients		
→ 2 cups of water		→ 2 tbsp. of lemon juice
→ 1 cup of quinoa		→ 1 cup of raisins
→ 2 cups of apple juice		→ Salt
→ 2 tsp. of vanilla extract		→ 1 tsp. of ground cinnamon

Direction

Rinse the quinoa deeply inside a sieve. Let it to drain, and combine quinoa and water inside a medium pot. Over high temperature, bring to one boil. Top the pan with cover, reduce heat to slow, and let to simmer for fifteen min or till all water has been absorbed & quinoa is soft. Combine the apple juice, lemon juice, raisins, cinnamon, & salt in a mixing bowl. Cover and continue to cook for another 15 minutes. Add the vanilla essence and mix well. Warm the dish before serving.

SAUSAGES & ALMOND MILK

Prep time: 5mins   **Cook time: 20mins**

Servings: 20

Nutritional information:

Per serving: Kcal 155, Fat: 10g, Carbs: 7g, Protein: 7g

Ingredients

→ 2 ½ tbsp. of Worcestershire sauce

→ 2 pounds of breakfast sausage

→ 1 cube of beef bouillon

→ 3 tsp. of black pepper, ground

→ 1 cup of flour all-purpose

→ 1 tsp. of ground nutmeg

→ 1 tsp. of salt

→ 4 cups of almond milk

Direction

In a big pan on moderate heat, break up the sausage. Cook for 3-5 minutes, or until the edges begin to brown. Allow your Worcestershire sauce to warm up before mixing the beef bouillon & nutmeg. Cook, stirring occasionally until the sausage is not pink, 3-5 minutes longer. Lower the heat and slowly add the flour. Cook, tossing regularly, till the flour has entirely absorbed and coated the sausage. Cook for another 1-2 mins. Pour in the almond milk slowly, stirring frequently, until the gravy thickens, about 12 minutes. If the mixture is too thick, add a bit extra almond milk. Salt & pepper to taste. Stir constantly until the gravy achieves the desired thickness. Take off the heat and set aside to cool. Season to taste, then adjust seasonings as needed.

Scrambled Tuscan Tofu

Prep time: 5mins   **Cook time: 25mins**

Servings: 4

Nutritional information:

Per serving: Kcal 461, Fat: 31g, Carbs: 27g, Protein: 20g

Ingredients

→ 1 tbsp of garlic powder

→ ¼ cup of nutritional yeast

→ ½ tsp of turmeric

→ 1 tsp of black pepper

→ 1 tsp of black salt

→ ½ cube of bouillon cube no-chicken or vegetable bouillon1 tsp

→ 1 cup of fresh spinach

→ 1 tbsp of butter non-dairy or coconut oil flavored

→ 1 cup of water

→ 1 small chopped onion

→ 2 thinly sliced green onion

→ 2 packages of tofu

→ 1 tbsp of finely chopped, fresh dill

Direction

Combine garlic powder, yeast, turmeric, pepper, salt, bouillon, & water in a bowl or mixer. Pulse or mix until smooth & lump-free. Put it aside. Heat the oil inside a moderate saucepan on moderate heat. Sauté onions in pan until they are transparent, approximately 3 to 5 minutes. Put tofu to a pan after crumbling it with the hands. 3 min in the oven add the broth mix to your pan and the tofu, then simmer for four minutes without stirring. Cook, stirring periodically until all of the fluid has evaporated. Approximately 5-8 min. Green onion, spinach, fresh dill, and all-purpose spices Sauté for 3 minutes, or until the greens are cooked. Add more dill and/or chili flakes as desired.

5.2 Lunch

ANCIENT SALMON BURGERS

Prep time: 10mins   **Cook time: 18mins**

Servings: 6

Nutritional information:

Per serving: Kcal 384, Fat: 12g, Carbs: 28g, Protein: 37g

Ingredients

→ 1/2 cup of fresh breadcrumb

→ 2 lbs. of salmon, center cut boneless and skinless

→ 1 lightly beaten egg

→ 6 hot dog buns, sesame seed toasted

→ 1 finely grated lemon zest

→ 2 thinly sliced scallions

→ 2 tbsp. of chives finely snipped

→ 1 tbsp. of olive oil extra virgin

→ 1 tbsp. of minced garlic

→ 1 tsp. of red wine vinegar

→ salt

→ 1 -2 dash of Tabasco sauce

→ Ground pepper

Direction

With the knife, coarsely cut the fish. Put in a stick blender and process on & off until a coarse texture is achieved; don't really over-process. Except for the buns & garnishes, lightly mix salmon in the other ingredients. Form six patties with a diameter of 3 inches as well as a thickness of 1 inch. For grilling, preheat the coals or the gas grill. Vegetable oil should be brushed on the grill. Flip the burgers gently after 3-4 minutes on each side, or till just done thoroughly. Serve warm on toasted buns using your preference of toppings.

Baked Mahi

Nutritional information:

Per serving: Kcal 155, Fat: 10g, Carbs: 7g, Protein: 7g

Ingredients	
→ 1 juiced lemon	→ 1 cup of mayonnaise
→ breadcrumbs	→ 1/4 tsp. of ground black pepper
→ 2 lbs 4 fillets mahi mahi	→ 1/4 cup of chopped white onion
→ 1/4 tsp. of garlic salt	

Direction

Preheat the oven to 425 degrees Fahrenheit. Place the fish on a baking dish after rinsing it. Drizzle lemon juice over the fish, then season with pepper and salt. Spread mayonnaise & chopped onions on the fish. Cook for 30 min at 425°F using breadcrumbs on top.

Baked Sardines with Wilted Rocket Salad

Prep time: 10mins   **Cook time: 15mins**

Servings: 5

Nutritional information:

Per serving: Kcal 179, Fat: 21g, Carbs: 0g, Protein: 0g

Ingredients

→ 16 fresh innards removed sardines

→ Lemon wedges

→ 2 trimmed baby arugula bunches

→ Kosher salt & black pepper

→ 2 teaspoons olive oil extra-virgin

Direction

Prepare griddle on the stovetop or an outside grill. Shake off any extra water after rinsing the arugula. Place everything on a big dish and put it aside. Clean the scales by rinsing the sardines in ice water and wiping them off. Dry with a clean cloth. Mix the sardines with olive oil in a basin to coat. Grill for 2-3 minutes each side over extremely hot coals and heat, or till sardines become crispy & golden. Salt & pepper to taste. Transfer to arugula-lined tray as soon as possible and serve using lemon wedges.

BAKED SOLE

Nutritional information:

Per serving: Kcal 247, Fat: 17g, Carbs: 7g, Protein: 17g

Ingredients		
→ Coarse salt	→ 3 tbsp of breadcrumbs
→ 1 lb. of sole fillets	→ ¼ cup lemon juice
→ ¼ cup of vegetable oil	→ 3 tbsp Parmesan cheese grated
→ ½ tsp of paprika	

Direction

Preheat the oven to 350 ° Fahrenheit. Sprinkle salt on sole fillets. Whisk together the oil & lemon juice inside a small bowl. Fill a baking dish halfway with the batter. Add fish to the pan, then coat every fillet in the lemon-oil combination. Breadcrumbs should be uniformly distributed on the fillets, followed by the cheese & paprika. Bake approximately 15 to 20 minutes, or till the fish readily flakes when using a fork. Based on the width of your fillets, the cooking times can vary. Serve and have fun.

BROCCOLI WITH CHICKEN

Prep time: 15mins   **Cook time: 20mins**

Servings: 3

Nutritional information:

Per serving: Kcal 356, Fat: 7g, Carbs: 40g, Protein: 33g

Ingredients

→ ¼ cup of brown sugar

→ ⅔ cup of soy sauce

→ ½ tsp. of ground ginger

→ 3 cups of broccoli florets

→ 2 tbsp. of water

→ 1 pinch of red pepper flakes

→ 2 tbsp. of cornstarch

→ 3 boneless, skinless chicken breasts

→ 2 tsp. of vegetable oil

→ 1 sliced onion,

Direction

To absorb the sugar, whisk together brown sugar, ginger, soy sauce, & red pepper flakes in a mixing dish. In a mixing bowl, combine the water & cornstarch; stir till cornstarch is fully dissolved. In a medium saucepan, heat the oil on high heat.5-7 minutes in heated oil, fry chicken & onion till chicken is just not pink in the middle and onion is soft. Stir broccoli into chicken & onion mixture and cook for 5 mins, or till broccoli is heated. The chicken & vegetable combination should be pushed to the edge of the pan. Fill the empty section of the pan with soy sauce mixture. Mix the cornstarch mixture into mixture of soy sauce till it becomes a uniform color. Return the chicken & veggies to the middle of the pan, then cook for another 5 minutes, or till sauce thickens & coats the meat and veg.

Brussels Sprouts Creamy Soup

Nutritional information:

Per serving: Kcal 122, Fat: 8g, Carbs: 11g, Protein: 4g

Ingredients	
→ 1/3 cup of chopped carrot	→ 2 minced cloves garlic
→ 1-pound Brussels sprouts 1/3 cup chopped celery	→ 1/2 tsp. of dried thyme
	→ 1/8 tsp. of salt
→ 1/3 cup of chopped onion	→ 1/4 tsp. of black pepper
→ 1 tsp. of Dijon mustard	→ 3 tbsp. of apple cider
→ 1/2 cup of heavy cream	→ 4 cups of chicken broth

Direction

Inside a medium saucepan, combine the Brussels sprouts, carrot, celery, onion, mustard, garlic, thyme, salt, and pepper. Combine the broth & cider in a mixing bowl. Bring to one boil in a saucepan on moderate heat. Simmer about 10 to 15 minutes, or till veggies are tender and cooked thoroughly. Blend everything together with an immersion blender until it reaches the appropriate consistency. Cook for several minutes more, till the cream has thickened somewhat.

CHICKEN & EGGPLANT

Prep time: 50mins   **Cook time: 30mins**

Servings: 5

Nutritional information:

Per serving: Kcal 336, Fat: 10g, Carbs: 26g, Protein: 35g

Ingredients

→ 3 tbsp. of olive oil

→ 3 eggplants

→ 6 boneless, skinless chicken breasts

→ salt & pepper

→ 2 tbsp. of tomato paste

→ 1 diced onion

→ 2 tsp. of dried oregano

→ ½ cup of water

Direction

Soak eggplant slices for thirty min in a large saucepan of mildly salted water. Remove the eggplant from the saucepan and gently spray olive oil on it. Put in a baking dish after sautéing or

grilling until golden brown. Set it aside. In a big pan, cook diced chicken & onion on moderate flame. Stir in the tomato paste & water, then cover, and cook for 10mins on low flame. Preheat the oven to 400 ° Fahrenheit. Over the eggplant, pour the chicken and tomato mixture. Cover with tinfoil and sprinkle with salt, oregano, and pepper. Cook for twenty minutes in a pre-heated oven.

CHICKEN PENNE PASTA

Prep time: 15mins   **Cook time: 1hr 10mins**

Servings: 4

Nutritional information:

Per serving: Kcal 572, Fat: 17g, Carbs: 37g, Protein: 64g

Ingredients

→ ¼ cup of brown sugar	→ ½ onion
→ 2 cups of pomegranate juice	→ 1 whole chicken
→ 1 tablespoon of cider vinegar	→ 1 ¼ tsp. of salt
→ 1 tbsp. of lime juice	→ ½ tsp. of dried rosemary
→ 2 smashed and peeled cloves garlic	→ ½ tsp. of black pepper
→ 1 lime	→ 1 bay leaf

Direction

Preheat the oven to 400° Fahrenheit. Inside a saucepan, combine the brown sugar, pomegranate juice, garlic and vinegar. On moderate flame, bring to one boil. Cook, stirring periodically, for approximately 10 minutes, or until the mixture has been reduced to three fourth cup. Remove from heat & remove your garlic, and then whisk in some lime juice & set aside for 5 minutes to cool. 6 tbsp pomegranate syrup, let aside. Insert onions, 1/2 tsp salt, pepper, bay leaf, and rosemary in chicken cavity after poking numerous holes in lemon with fork. Tie the legs along with kitchen thread, season its skin with additional salt, and place the chicken inside a roasting pan, chest side up. Roast the chicken, drizzling using pomegranate syrup after twenty minutes, till a thermometer put into thickest portions of all parts reads 165 ° F., approximately one hour in total. Allow 10 minutes for the chicken to rest before cutting. Drizzle with the remaining pomegranate syrup before serving.

CURRY SALMON WITH BLACK CABBAGE

Prep time: 7mins   **Cook time: 23mins**

Servings: 4

Nutritional information:

Per serving: Kcal 506, Fat: 25g, Carbs: 18g, Protein: 50g

Ingredients

- → 1/4 tsp of Salt
- → 4 small Skinless Boneless Salmon fillets
- → 1 1/2 tbsp of Curry Powder
- → 2 stalks of minced Green Onions
- → 2 tsp minced Ginger Root
- → 1 1/4 lbs. of chopped Black Cabbage
- → 1 cup Chicken Broth Low Sodium
- → 1/4 tsp Red Pepper Flakes Crushed

Direction

Preheat the oven to 425 degrees Fahrenheit. Rub some salt into the fish until it is completely dissolved. Let five min for the salmon to rest. On a dish, spread curry powder, then roll every salmon fillet in it until it is uniformly covered. Place the salmon onto your baking sheet, then bake for 8-10 minutes at 425°F. Slice Napa cabbage in bite-sized chunks and lay aside, whereas the salmon bakes. Put chicken broth & ginger in a pan and broil. Cover & bring to one boil with the cabbage & red pepper flakes. Reduce the heat to low and cook for 3-5 minutes, or till the cabbage is soft. Combine the cabbage and green onions inside a mixing bowl. Serve salmon over a cabbage bed.

Eggplant Steak with Feta Cheese, Black Olives, Roasted Peppers and Chickpeas

Prep time: 25mins   **Cook time: 5mins**

Servings: 4

Nutritional information:

Per serving: Kcal 460, Fat: 16g, Carbs: 54g, Protein: 18g

Ingredients	
→ 1 1/2 cups of drained garbanzo beans	→ 4 6 1/2" rounds pita breads
→ 1 lb. of eggplant	→ 2 tbsp. of olive oil
→ 2 medium sized red bell peppers	→ 1 bunch of fresh oregano
→ 1/2 cup pitted black olives	→ 4 tsp. of balsamic vinegar
→ 1/4 lb. of crumbled feta cheese	→ Balsamic marinade
→ 2 tbsp. fresh chopped oregano,	→ 1 tbsp. of tamari sauce
	→ 1 tbsp. of balsamic vinegar
→ black pepper	→ 1/4 tsp. of black pepper
→ salt	→ 2 minced cloves garlic

Direction

To create the marinade, put all of the ingredients in a mixing bowl, gently drizzle in the olive oil, and whisk vigorously to incorporate. Set it aside. Preheat the grill or the oven broiler. Cut the eggplant into 4 1/2" slices lengthwise. Brush the marinade on the meat. 2 mins on every side, or till tender and not soft, grill/broil the eggplant. Remove the steaks from the heat and put one on every serving platter. In a mixing bowl, combine chickpeas, feta, red peppers, black olives, & oregano. Season with salt & pepper, and mix well to blend. Stir in part of the marinade once more. Pita bread should be toasted or grilled, then sliced into pie-shaped slices and placed aside. Place 1-2 scoops of the pepper-olive mix on top of the eggplant steak, with a few of the mixture pooling on the dish. Place many pita wedges onto a platter and drizzle some balsamic vinegar. Top with extra oregano. Repeat with the remaining ingredients till all of them have been utilized. Serve right away.

GREEK CHICKEN & BEANS

Prep time: 2mins **Cook time: 4hrs**

Servings: 4

Nutritional information:

Per serving: Kcal 324, Fat: 18g, Carbs: 7g, Protein: 26g

<table>
<tr><td rowspan="2">Ingredients</td><td>

→ 2 large chopped tomatoes

→ 1 pound trimmed green beans

→ 1 medium chopped onion

→ 1/4 cup of fresh dill snipped

→ 1 cup of chicken broth
</td><td>

→ 2-3 tbsp. of lemon juice Lemon wedges & snipped dill

→ 4 chicken thighs bone-in

→ 2 minced garlic cloves

→ 3/4 tsp. of salt

→ 1 tbsp. of olive oil

→ 1/4 tsp. of pepper
</td></tr>
</table>

Direction

Inside a 5- or 6-quart slow cooker, mix the first seven ingredients. Serve with chicken on top. Drizzle extra oil and season with salt & pepper to taste. Cook over low for 4-6 hrs, covered, till a thermometer placed in the chicken registers 170°-175°. Preheat the oven to broil. In a roasting pan, place the chicken on oiled rack. 3-four hours, broil 4-6 inches from fire till golden brown. Serve with the lemon wedges, bean mixture, plus fresh dill, if preferred.

Grilled Codfish

Prep time: 10mins   **Cook time: 10mins**

Servings: 4

Nutritional information:

Per serving: Kcal 152, Fat: 6g, Carbs: 2g, Protein: 20g

Ingredients

→ 1 tbsp. of Cajun seasoning

→ 2 fillets cod

→ ½ tsp. of lemon pepper

→ 2 tablespoons white part green onion chopped

→ ¼ tsp. of black pepper

→ ¼ tsp. of salt

→ 1 juiced lemon

→ 2 tbsp. of butter

Direction

Inside a grill, stack roughly fifteen charcoal briquettes in a pyramid form. If desired, gently mist the coals using lighter fluid, then let them soak for one min before igniting with a flame. Let ten mins for the heat to be transferred to all coals prior to actually spreading briquettes out onto the grill; wait for the coals to burn till a thin coating of white ash coats them. Grates should be lightly oiled. Cajun spice, salt, lemon pepper, and black pepper are sprinkled over both surfaces of the fish. Place the fish on a platter and set it away. In a medium saucepan, melt butter on moderate heat, add lemon juice & green onion, then simmer for 3 minutes, or till onion is cooked. Put cod on greased grill grates & cook till browned and flaky, approximately 3 minutes each side; baste periodically in butter mixture while cooking. Allow it for a five-minute resting period after removing the fish from the heat.

GRILLED GARLIC LAMB CHOP

Prep time: 15mins   **Cook time: 10mins**

Servings: 4

Nutritional information:

Per serving: Kcal 519, Fat: 44g, Carbs: 2g, Protein: 25g

Ingredients	
→ 4 minced cloves garlic	→ 1 tablespoon chopped rosemary fresh
→ 2 pounds of rib chops or lamb loin thick cut	→ 1 lemon zest
→ 1/4 cup of olive oil	→ 1/2 teaspoon black pepper
→ 1 1/4 teaspoon of kosher salt	

Direction

Inside a measuring container, mix the garlic, salt, rosemary, pepper, olive oil and lemon zest. Spoon the marinade on lamb chops and turn them over to properly coat them. Refrigerate the chops for one hour, covered. Grill the chops of lamb for 7 to 10 minutes over medium heat, or till they reach an internal temperature of 135 degrees F. Let the chops to sit for five min on a platter covered with tinfoil for serving.

GRILLED LEMON SALMON

Prep time: 10mins   **Cook time: 15mins**

Servings: 6

Nutritional information:

Per serving: Kcal 280, Fat: 17g, Carbs: 7g, Protein: 23g

Ingredients

→ 1/2 tsp. of lemon-pepper seasoning

→ 2 teaspoons of snipped dill, otherwise 3/4 tsp. of dill weed

→ 1/2 tsp. of salt

→ 1 fillet of salmon

→ 1/4 teaspoon of garlic powder

→ 1/4 cup of brown sugar packed

→ 2 slices of onion

→ 3 tablespoons of canola oil

→ 3 tablespoons of chicken broth

→ 3 tablespoons of soy sauce reduced-sodium

→ 1 small thinly sliced lemon

→ 3 tablespoons of green onions finely chopped

Direction

Lemon pepper, dill, salt if preferred, & garlic powder are sprinkled over the fish. Mix broth, brown sugar, oil, green onions and soy sauce in a big Ziplock bag; add your salmon. Close the bag, then coat it. Cover and chill for one hour, flipping halfway through. Drain and toss out the marinade. Grill salmon skin piece down on moderate flame, then top with lemon & onion slices. Cook, covered, for 15 to 20 minutes, or till the fish readily flakes with your fork.

Grilled Tuna

Prep time: 10mins   **Cook time: 11mins**

Servings: 4

Nutritional information:

Per serving: Kcal 200, Fat: 8g, Carbs: 4g, Protein: 27g

Ingredients	
→ ¼ cup of soy sauce	→ 1 tablespoon of lemon juice
→ ¼ cup of orange juice	→ ½ teaspoon of fresh oregano chopped
→ 2 tablespoons of olive oil	→ 1 minced clove garlic
→ 4 tuna steaks (4 ounce)	→ ½ teaspoon of black pepper
→ 2 tablespoons of fresh parsley chopped	

Direction

Combine the soy sauce, orange juice, lemon juice, olive oil, parsley, oregano, garlic, and pepper in a big non-reactive pan. Turn tuna steaks in marinade to cover them. Chill for about 30 min after covering. Preheat the grill to high. Grease the grill grate well. Cook until 5-6 minutes on each side, then flip and coat with marinade. Cook for another 5 minutes, or until desired doneness is reached. Any leftover marinade should be discarded.

Lamb Chops

Prep time: 10mins   **Cook time: 10mins**

Servings: 4

Nutritional information:

Per serving: Kcal 506, Fat: 37g, Carbs: 1g, Protein: 43g

Ingredients

→ Salt and ground pepper	→ 3 tablespoons olive oil extra-virgin
→ 8 lamb loin chops 1/2-inch-thick	→ 2 tablespoons of lemon juice
→ dried thyme	→ 3 tablespoons of water
→ red pepper crushed	→ 2 tablespoons of parsley minced
→ 10 small halved garlic cloves	

Direction

Sprinkle the lamb using pepper and salt, as well as a thin sprinkling of thyme. Warm olive oil inside a big pan until it shimmers. Cook your lamb chops & garlic over fairly high heat for 3 minutes, or till the chops become browned just on bottom.

Cook, turning the chops & garlic occasionally, until browned, approximately 2 minutes more for moderate meat. Leave the garlic inside the pan while transferring the chops to dishes. Cook, trying to scrape any browned pieces clinging to the base of the pan, till the water, parsley, lemon juice, and smashed red pepper are sizzling, approximately 1 minute. Toss lamb chops immediately with the garlic & pan sauce.

LIVER WITH AVOCADO & SHALLOTS

Prep time: 5mins   **Cook time: 8mins**

Servings: 5

Nutritional information:

Per serving: Kcal 531, Fat: 49g, Carbs: 21g, Protein: 4g

Ingredients

→ 2 medium quartered and peeled avocados

→ 8 slices (thin 1 and a half ounce slices) of calf liver

→ 1 tbsp. of grated parmesan cheese

→ 1/2 cup of flour

→ 12 tbsp. of butter

→ 2 tsp. of salt

→ 1 tbsp. of chopped shallots

→ 1 lemon

Direction

Sprinkle the liver & avocado slices using flour as well as a pinch of salt. 2 sauté pans should be hot. 4 tbsp butter, melted in each. Quickly sauté the slices of liver in one pan & avocado slices in the second pan for approximately 1/2 min on every side. Alternate the liver slices and diced avocado on a hot platter. Butter, lemon juice, chopped shallots, & Parmesan cheese inside the pan where the liver is sautéed. Cook, stirring constantly, till the butter is gently browned. Spread the sauce quickly on the liver & avocados.

MEATLOAF OF LAMB

Prep time: 15mins　　　　**Cook time: 60mins**

Servings: 1

Nutritional information:

Per serving: Kcal 483, Fat: 29g, Carbs: 13g, Protein: 40g

Ingredients

- → 1/2 cup of dry breadcrumbs
- → 2 eggs
- → 1/2 tsp. of salt
- → 1 lb. of beef
- → 1/4 tsp. of black pepper
- → 1 lb. of lamb
- → 1 medium chopped onion
- → 2 tbsp. of olive oil
- → 1 tablespoon of Worcestershire sauce
- → 4 minced garlic cloves,
- → 1 teaspoon of dried basil
- → 1 teaspoon of dried thyme
- → 1/2 cup of ketchup, otherwise 1/2 cup of tomato paste

Direction

Preheat oven to 350 ° Fahrenheit. Sauté the garlic, onion, thyme, & basil inside the olive oil to a large pan till the onion is tender and nearly brown. Remove the skillet from the heat & set aside to cool. In a large mixing basin, crack eggs and whisk them together. Combine the salt, breadcrumbs, and pepper in a mixing bowl. Combine the ground meats with the garlic, onion, & herbs that have been cooled. Combine Worcestershire sauce & ketchup in a mixing bowl. Combine all ingredients and bake in a prepared loaf pan. Make sure it's securely packed. Preheat oven to 350°F and bake for about 60 to 65 minutes. Allow five min for cooling. Drain the fat before serving.

OLD LAMB GRANNY BURGER

Prep time: 50mins **Cook time: 10mins**

Servings: 6

Nutritional information:

Per serving: Kcal 742, Fat: 33g, Carbs: 70g, Protein: 37g

Ingredients

- → 1 cup of stale breadcrumbs
- → 500g Coles Lamb Mince
- → 1 Egg
- → 1/4 cup chopped fresh mint
- → 1 coarsely grated brown onion,
- → 1/2 mini finely shredded savoy cabbage
- → 1 carrot, peeled
- → 1/2 mini finely shredded red cabbage
- → Six Coles Hamburger Rolls
- → 2 tbsp toasted pine nuts
- → 1 tsp of Dijon mustard
- → 1/4 cup of mayonnaise whole-egg
- → 6 slices of Castello Burger Blue cheese
- → One Granny Smith apple

Direction

In a mixing bowl, combine the mince, egg, breadcrumbs, onion, & mint. Season. Divide the mixture into 6 equal parts. Make a 12cm patty out of each half. Place on a serving dish. Wrap with saran wrap and chill for 30 minutes to let flavors to meld. In a mixing bowl, combine the cabbage, pine nuts, carrot, mayonnaise, & mustard. Season. Preheat a grill/chargrill to high heat. Cook the patties for three minutes on every side or till done. Serve some blue cheese on top. Cook about 1 minute or until the cheese melts. Place on a platter to cool. Cook about 1 minute on every side, or until gently browned, on the grill. Heat the cut surface of rolls for 1 minute or till gently browned on the grill. Put on plates to serve. Coleslaw, patties and apple go on top. Sandwich with the tops of the rolls and serve right away.

PAN-GRILLED MINCED PORK BURGERS

Prep time: 15mins   Cook time: 10mins

Servings: 4

Nutritional information:

Per serving: Kcal 693, Fat: 47g, Carbs: 40g, Protein: 27g

Ingredients	
→ 1 banana	→ ½ cup of mayonnaise
→ 2 red sweet peppers	→ 1 pound of ground pork
→ jalapeño or chile pepper	→ 4 bread rounds or flat bread
→ 1 tablespoon of soy or Worcestershire sauce	→ 8 ounces fresh mushrooms sliced

Direction

Half of the peppers should be cut into rings and left aside. Chop what's left. Mix pork, chopped peppers, 2 tsp Worcestershire sauce, and 2 tsp cracked black pepper inside a mixing bowl. Form the burgers into 4 3/4-inch wide patties. Cook patties in a big heated skillet on moderate heat for 10-12 minutes, turning once. Cover and transfer onto plates. Cook for 3 minutes in the same pan with the pepper rings & mushrooms; season with salt. Wrap the bread in towels and set aside. Microwave for thirty seconds on Maximum. To make the sauce, whisk together the mayonnaise, the leftover Worcestershire sauce, & black pepper. Top the burgers with some pepper-mushroom mixture and serve. Please pass the sauce. This recipe serves 4 people.

Pasta & Shrimps

Prep time: 10mins   **Cook time: 10mins**

Servings: 4

Nutritional information:

Per serving: Kcal 511, Fat: 19g, Carbs: 57g, Protein: 21g

Ingredients	
→ 1 pound of deveined and peeled shrimp	→ 2 tablespoons of parsley leaves, fresh and chopped
→ 8 ounces of fettuccine	→ 1/2 teaspoon of dried oregano
→ Kosher salt & black pepper	→ 2 cups of baby arugula
→ 4 minced cloves garlic	→ 1/2 teaspoon of red pepper flakes crushed
→ 8 tablespoons of unsalted butter	→ 1/4 cup of Parmesan freshly grated

Direction

Cook pasta as per package directions in a big saucepan of simmering salted water; drain thoroughly. Set aside the shrimp that have been seasoned with salt & pepper. In a big pan, melt 2 tbsp butter on moderate flame. Cook, stirring regularly, until the garlic, red pepper flakes and oregano are aromatic, approximately 1-2 minutes. Cook, tossing occasionally, till shrimp are pink, approximately 2-3 min; put aside. In the same pan, melt the extra 6 tbsp butter. 2 minutes after adding the pasta, arugula, & Parmesan, stir until the arugula starts to wilt. Add the shrimp and mix well. Serve warm with parsley on top, if preferred.

Pork & Marsala Wine

Prep time: 10mins   **Cook time: 20mins**

Servings: 4

Nutritional information:

Per serving: Kcal 455, Fat: 27g, Carbs: 18g, Protein: 17g

Ingredients

- → ¼ teaspoon of salt
- → ⅓ cup flour all-purpose
- → ¼ teaspoon of garlic salt
- → ½ teaspoon of dried oregano
- → ¾ teaspoon of garlic powder
- → 1 cup of Marsala wine
- → 1 pound of pork loin chops, pounded thin boneless
- → ¼ cup of olive oil
- → 3 tablespoons of butter
- → 1 teaspoon garlic minced
- → 2 cups fresh mushrooms sliced

Direction

In a large mixing bowl, combine flour, garlic salt, salt, garlic powder, & oregano. Toss in the pork chops until thoroughly coated. In a big skillet, melt butter & olive oil on moderate flame. Cook, turning periodically until the pork is brown on each side in a thin layer in a pan. Stir slightly after adding the mushrooms & garlic. Scrape the bottom of the pan to release any brown pieces before adding the wine. Cover & cook over moderate heat for 15 minutes, or till meat is tender & sauce has thickened. If the sauce is overly thick, thin it down with a splash of wine.

Pork Chops with Sage

Prep time: 10mins   **Cook time: 55mins**

Servings: 6

Nutritional information:

Per serving: Kcal 159, Fat: 8g, Carbs: 1g, Protein: 20g

Ingredients	
→ 1 teaspoon of dried sage → 2 teaspoons of salt → 2 cubes of beef bouillon → 1 teaspoon of ground black pepper	→ 2 tablespoons of butter → 6 bone-in pork chops → 1 cup of water

Direction

In a mixing dish, combine the sage, salt, & black pepper and massage both surfaces of the chop. In a big pan on moderate high heat, melt butter or margarine and cook the chop for 5mins each side, or till nicely browned. Meanwhile, put the water & bouillon in a small separate pot over high temperature and whisk till the bouillon mixes. Put this on the chops, lower to the slow heat setting, cover, and cook for 45min.

PORK CURRY WITH OLIVES, APRICOTS & CAULIFLOWER

Prep time: 15mins   **Cook time: 20mins**

Servings: 5

Nutritional information:

Per serving: Kcal 380, Fat: 22g, Carbs: 20g, Protein: 30g

Ingredients

- → 1/4 cup olive oil extra-virgin
- → 8 skinless, boneless chicken thighs
- → 1 Tbs. of apple cider vinegar
- → 1 tsp. of smoked paprika
- → 4 tsp. of curry powder
- → 1/2 tsp. of ground cinnamon
- → Kosher salt
- → 1/4 tsp. of cayenne pepper
- → 1 head cauliflower
- → 1 large sized lemon, 4-6 wedges
- → 1 cup green olives, pitted
- → 3/4 cup of dried apricots, coarsely chopped
- → 1/3 cup fresh cilantro chopped

Direction

Toss the chicken thighs using vinegar, 2 tablespoons oil, 2 teaspoons curry powder, 1/2 teaspoon paprika, cayenne, cinnamon, and 3/4 teaspoon salt inside a medium mixing basin. Chill for about eight hours or up to night if covered. Preheat oven to 450 degrees Fahrenheit and place a rack inside the middle. Using parchment paper, line a rimmed baking sheet. Toss cauliflower in your pan using the leftover 2 tablespoons oil, 2 teaspoons curry powder, 1/2 teaspoon paprika, & 3/4 teaspoon salt, turning to coat. Spread the apricots & olives in a thin layer on top. Take your chicken thighs out from marinade, twist them, returning to its original form, and equally distribute them over top of cauliflower. Roast for approximately 35 minutes, flipping the pan midway through, till cauliflower browns, as well as chicken, is cooked through. Toss cauliflower mix with drippings of pan after taking the chicken out from the saucepan. Serves the chicken & cauliflower combination with lime wedges just on side, garnished with cilantro.

QUICK HALIBUT DISH

Prep time: 5mins   **Cook time: 15mins**

Servings: 2

Nutritional information:

Per serving: Kcal 184, Fat: 6g, Carbs: 2g, Protein: 30g

Ingredients	
→ 1 tsp of olive oil	→ Juice half lemon
→ 2 5oz skin-on, boneless halibut fillets	→ 2 tsp of lemon zest
→ 1 large minced clove garlic,	→ 1 tbsp of flat leaf parsley chopped
→ Pinch of sea salt & black pepper	

Direction

Preheat the oven to 400 degrees Fahrenheit. Place the halibut skin piece down in a huge nonstick cake pan and sprinkling with oil. Garlic, lemon zest, parsley, and 2 tablespoons lemon juice are equally distributed over top. Salt & pepper to taste. Preheat oven to 350°F and bake for 12-15 minutes, or till halibut flakes readily when checked with a fork. Serve with the leftover lemon juice drizzled over top.

RAISINS, GARBANZOS AND SPINACH PASTA

Prep time: 15mins   **Cook time: 20mins**

Servings: 4

Nutritional information:

Per serving: Kcal 613, Fat: 12g, Carbs: 104g, Protein: 22g

Ingredients	
→ 1 package of linguine pasta (16 ounce)	→ 3 large diced and seeded tomatoes
→ 1 tbsp. of sea salt	→ 1 teaspoon of fresh marjoram, chopped
→ 2 tablespoons of olive oil, extra-virgin	→ 1 can (15 ounce) of garbanzo beans
→ 1 bag of leaves of baby spinach, (10 ounce) chopped	→ ½ teaspoon of red pepper flakes
→ ¼ cup Pecorino-Romano cheese, freshly grated	→ black pepper
→ 2 minced cloves garlic	

Direction

Bring a big saucepan of water to one boil with 2 tablespoons sea salt. Boil linguine for 11 minutes, or until soft but firm when you take a bite; drain, saving half cup water. In a medium saucepan, heat the olive oil on moderate flame. In a heated skillet, cook & stir garlic till fragrant, approximately one minute. Increase the heat to intermediate and add the tomatoes, spinach, & garbanzo beans; then cook & stir for another 1 to 2 minutes, just until the spinach starts to wilt. Add the remaining teaspoon of sea salt, black pepper, marjoram, & red pepper to the spinach mixture. Reduce the heat to just a low setting. Drain linguine and toss it with the mixture of spinach to cover it evenly. To reach the desired degree of wetness in dish, add more olive oil or leftover pasta water. Pecorino-Romano cheese is sprinkled on top.

Seared Calf's Liver

Prep time: 5mins   **Cook time: 5mins**

Servings: 2

Nutritional information:

Per serving: Kcal 687, Fat: 20g, Carbs: 74g, Protein: 48g

Ingredients	
→ butter & nut oil	→ few drops balsamic vinegar
→ salt & fresh pepper	→ 1 tbsp of capers
→ 2 slices of calf's liver	

Direction

In a pan, melt the butter with a dash of nut oil. Cook the liver slices over a high temperature until brown. On every side, cook for a minute or two. Then season using pepper and salt. Place them on 2 heated plates right immediately. Return frying pan to the ring, pour a butter, just several drops balsamic vinegar, and also the capers, and spoon this mixture on the liver gently.

Spanish Cod

Prep time: 20mins   **Cook time: 15mins**

Servings: 6

Nutritional information:

Per serving: Kcal 170, Fat: 6g, Carbs: 6g, Protein: 21g

Ingredients

→ 1 tablespoon of olive oil	→ fifteen cherry tomatoes
→ 1 tablespoon of butter	→ ¼ cup of coarsely chopped and drained Italian vegetable salad, deli marinated
→ ¼ cup onion finely chopped	
→ 1 cup of tomato sauce	→ ½ cup green olives chopped
→ 2 tablespoons fresh garlic chopped	→ 1 dash of black pepper
→ 6 fillets of cod fillets	→ 1 dash of paprika
	→ 1 dash of cayenne pepper

Direction

In a big skillet, melt butter & olive oil on moderate flame. Cook, stirring occasionally, until onions & garlic are somewhat soft, taking careful not to overdo the garlic. Bring the tomato sauce & cherry tomatoes to one simmer. Sprinkle with cayenne pepper, black pepper, & paprika and mix in olives as well as marinated veggies. Cook fillets with sauce about 5-8 minutes on moderate flame, or until readily flaked using a fork. Serve right away.

Spicy Chicken with Couscous

Prep time: 15mins   **Cook time: 15mins**

Servings: 4

Nutritional information:

Per serving: Kcal 486, Fat: 23g, Carbs: 45g, Protein: 28g

<table>
<tr><td rowspan="2">Ingredients</td><td>

→ 3 tbsp of olive oil

→ 250g of couscous

→ 1 onion chopped

→ 120g pack of fresh coriander

</td><td>

→ 85g almonds blanched

→ 2 large boneless skinless fillets of chicken breast, sliced

→ 100g ready-to-eat apricots

→ 1 tbsp paste of hot curry

</td></tr>
</table>

<table>
<tr><td>Direction</td><td>

Cook couscous in chicken stock as per package directions. In a skillet, heat some olive oil and sauté the onion about 2 to 3 minutes, or till softened. Stir in the fillets of chicken breast and cook for 5-6 minutes, or until they are tender. Cook for 60 seconds further after adding the roasted almonds and stirring in hot curry paste. Combine the apricots, couscous, and coriander in a mixing bowl. Toss until heated through, then top with plain yoghurt, if desired.

</td></tr>
</table>

Sweet Potato Curry Chickpeas and Spinach

Prep time: 10mins   **Cook time: 20mins**

Servings: 6

Nutritional information:

Per serving: Kcal 283, Fat: 21g, Carbs: 22g, Protein: 5g

Ingredients	
→ 1 chopped onion	→ 1 cup of baby spinach
→ 3 tablespoons of olive oil	→ 1 cubed sweet potato
→ 2 minced cloves garlic	→ 1 teaspoon of ground cumin
→ 1 can (15 ounce) drained chickpeas	→ 1 tablespoon of garam masala
→ 2 teaspoons ginger root minced	→ 1 teaspoon of ground turmeric
→ 1 can (14 ounce) coconut milk	→ ¼ teaspoon of red chili flakes
→ 1 can (14.5 ounce) tomatoes diced	→ ½ teaspoon of salt

Direction

Cook garlic, onion, and ginger inside a pan on moderate heat till softened, approximately 5 minutes. Combine chickpeas, coconut milk, tomatoes, & sweet potato in a large mixing bowl.

Bring to one boil, then lower to a slow heat and cook until the vegetables are soft, approximately 15 minutes. Garam masala, turmeric, cumin, salt and chili flakes are used to season. Just before serving, toss in the spinach.

TETRAZZINI OF BEEF

Prep time: 20mins   **Cook time: 30mins**

Servings: 6

Nutritional information:

Per serving: Kcal 631, Fat: 37g, Carbs: 34g, Protein: 38g

Ingredients

→ 1 small chopped onion

→ 1-1/2 pounds of ground beef

→ 1 (15 ounces) can of tomato sauce

→ 1/4 teaspoon of pepper

→ 1/4 cup Parmesan cheese grated

→ ½-1 teaspoon of salt

→ 1 (8 ounces) package of softened cream cheese

→ 1 cup of sour cream

→ 1 cup of 4 percent cottage cheese

→ 1 (7 ounces) package of thin spaghetti

→ 1/4 cup green onions thinly sliced

Direction

Cook beef & onion in a big pan on moderate heat until the meat is just not pink; drain. Boil it with the salt, tomato sauce, and pepper. Reduce heat to low and cook for 5 mins, uncovered. Cream together cottage cheese, cream cheese, & sour cream in a mixing basin until smooth. In a large mixing bowl, combine the onions, green pepper, and pasta. Place the mixture in a greased 2-1/2-quart baking dish. Add the beef mixture on top. Parmesan cheese should be sprinkled on top. Bake for about 30 to 35 minutes, at 350°F, or till bubbling.

THE BEST–BAKED POTATOES

Prep time: 1mins   **Cook time: 1 hr30mins**

Servings: 1

Nutritional information:

Per serving: Kcal 419, Fat: 24g, Carbs: 38g, Protein: 13g

Ingredients	
→ 1 teaspoon of olive oil	→ ½ teaspoon of salt
→ ¼ cup Cheddar cheese shredded	→ 1 pinch black pepper freshly ground
→ 1 medium sized baking potato	→ 2 teaspoons of butter

Direction

Preheat oven to 300°F. Scrub potato and penetrate the skin with a fork or knife numerous times. Apply olive oil to the skin before applying salt. Bake for about 90 mins, just until potato is somewhat tender and nicely browned, in a pre-heated oven. Serve the potato using butter & black pepper, sliced along the middle. If desired, grate some grated Cheddar cheese on top.

Vegan Fried Fish Tacos

Prep time: 40mins   **Cook time: 10mins**

Servings: 12

Nutritional information:

Per serving: Kcal 305, Fat: 17g, Carbs: 31g, Protein: 4g

Ingredients

→ 12 small flour or corn tortillas

→ 1 Recipe Beer Battered Vegan Fried Fish

→ 1/2 small shredded purple cabbage

→ 1/4 finely diced red or white onion

→ 2 finely diced roma tomatoes

→ 1/2 bunch of chopped fresh cilantro

→ vegan cheese crumbled

→ 1-2 diced or sliced avocados

→ 1 teaspoon of Sriracha hot sauce

→ 1-2 limes

→ 1 tablespoon lime juice

→ 1/2 cup of vegan mayo

→ 1/2 teaspoon of garlic powder

Direction

Make vegan fish first. Toss together all of the toppings of taco and put them aside. Whisk together the ingredients of sauce in a bowl till smooth. Set it aside. Heat the tortillas after the fish has been cooked. You may toast them rapidly in a dry skillet on moderate heat or wrap some in paper towels & microwave for one minute. Place just few slices of fish for each tortilla, then top with your favorite toppings and a sprinkle of sauce. Slice the fish into very few smaller parts if they are fairly big. Serve warm with lime wedges over the tacos.

Veggies & Salmon Kedgeree

Prep time: 5mins   **Cook time: 20mins**

Servings: 4

Nutritional information:

Per serving: Kcal 503, Fat: 11g, Carbs: 70g, Protein: 25g

<table>
<tr><td rowspan="3">Ingredients</td><td>→ 500g packet of vegetable mix, frozen</td><td>→ 2 150g salmon portions hot-smoked, flaked, skin removed</td></tr>
<tr><td>→ 1 1/2 cups of Basmati rice</td><td>→ 3 tsp of curry powder</td></tr>
<tr><td>→ 1 1/2 tbsp of vegetable oil</td><td>→ 4 thinly sliced green onions</td></tr>
</table>

Direction

Cook rice for 10-12 minutes in a pot of hot, salted water, or till just soft, adding veggies for the final 5 minutes. In a big, wide frying pan, heat the oil on moderate flame. Cook, stirring occasionally, for 3 min or till onion is softened. Toss with the curry powder. Cook for 1 min, stirring constantly, or until aromatic. Toss in the rice. To blend, stir everything together. Toss in the veggies and fish. Salt & pepper to taste. Heat for 2 - 3 mins, or until well heated. Serve.

5.3 Dinner

ASIAN WITH BLACK OLIVES

Prep time: 5mins   **Cook time: 0mins**

Servings: 4

Nutritional information:

Per serving: Kcal 177, Fat: 18g, Carbs: 6g, Protein: 1g

<table>
<tr><td rowspan="2">Ingredients</td><td>→ 150 g green olives pitted</td><td>→ 2 g bay leaf - dry or fresh</td></tr>
<tr><td>→ 150 g black olives pitted

→ 1 lemon

→ Salt & pepper</td><td>→ 2 tablespoon (26 g) extra virgin olive oil

→ ¼ tablespoon (2 g) oregano - dry or fresh</td></tr>
</table>

Direction

Drain olives and set aside. Combine with olive oil, which should be in a mixing dish. Roll a piece of lemon rind across your finger and thumb to bruise it. This allows citrus oil to be released from its skin. Squeeze 14 ounces of juice of lemon over the olives after cutting the lemon in two. 1 tiny garlic clove, peeled and minced, is added to the olives. Combine the herbs & bay leaf in a bowl. Salt & pepper to taste. Mix everything together well, preferably overnight, but you may eat it right away.

Baked Tilapia

Prep time: 5mins   **Cook time: 30mins**

Servings: 4

Nutritional information:

Per serving: Kcal 172, Fat: 3g, Carbs: 7g, Protein: 24g

Ingredients

→ 2 tsp. of butter

→ 1 package (16 ounce) cauliflower, frozen with red pepper and broccoli

→ 4-ounce (4) fillets tilapia

→ ¼ tsp. of Old Bay Seasoning TM

→ 1 sliced lemon

→ ½ tsp. of garlic salt

Direction

Preheat oven to 190 degrees F. Grease a baking dish. Dot your tilapia fillets using butter inside the baking dish. Sprinkle with garlic salt & Old Bay flavor. Add a lemon couple of slices to each one. Sprinkle the refrigerated mixed veggies gently with pepper and salt, then arrange them around the fish. Top the dish, then bake inside the preheated oven about 25-30 minutes, till the veggies are soft and fish flakes readily using a fork.

Baked Veggies with Pork

Prep time: 20mins   **Cook time: 30mins**

Servings: 8

Nutritional information:

Per serving: Kcal 234, Fat: 4g, Carbs: 33g, Protein: 26g

Ingredients

- → Cooking spray Vegetable
- → 1 ½ pounds of pork tenderloin boneless
- → 1 pound of peeled carrots
- → 1 medium sized onion
- → Sage sprigs, rosemary
- → 2 pounds of new potatoes

- → 1 tbsp. of olive oil
- → 1 tsp. of crushed dried sage
- → 2 tsp. of crushed dried rosemary
- → ¼ tsp. of pepper
- → ¼ tsp. of salt

Direction

Inside a skillet covered with nonstick spray, brown the pork on moderate flame. Arrange veggies around the meat in a baking dish covered with nonstick spray. Drizzle using olive oil, then equally sprinkle the rosemary and the next three ingredients. Bake, turning periodically, at 450°, about thirty min till a thermometer placed into the thickest section registers 165° and veggies are cooked. If desired, garnish.

Barbecued Spicy Chicken Burger

Prep time: 20mins   **Cook time: 10mins**

Servings: 1

Nutritional information:

Per serving: Kcal 238, Fat: 34g, Carbs: 12g, Protein: 56g

Ingredients

- → 40g pkt Grill Mates American BBQ Slow & Low Smokin' Texas BBQ Rub
- → 6 Fillets of Chicken Thigh
- → 2 tbsp of olive oil
- → 1 cup savoy cabbage shredded (80g)
- → 1 cup red cabbage shredded (80g)
- → Oven-baked chips
- → 1 coarsely grated carrot
- → 1/4 cup Packs (75g) a Egg Peri Mayo
- → 1 thinly sliced spring onion
- → 1/2 cup Grown Tomato Sauce(40g)
- → 6 toasted brioche burger buns

Direction

Preheat a grill/chargrill to high heat. Rub the chicken with the rub and just a little oil. Heat for 5 minutes on every side or till well done. Place on a platter to cool. Wrap foil around the dish. Allow for a 5-minute rest period. In a mixing bowl, combine the carrot, cabbage, mayonnaise and spring onion. Season. Toss everything together. Serve the bun bottoms on individual plates. Add the chicken, tomato sauce, bun tops, coleslaw mixture to the tops of the buns. Serve alongside the chips.

BEEF BURGER

Nutritional information:

Per serving: Kcal 472, Fat: 26g, Carbs: 28g, Protein: 31g

Ingredients	
→ 1 finely chopped and peeled onion	→ ketchup
→ ½ tbsp of olive oil	→ 4 slices of mature Cheddar
→ 1 500g-pack 15% fat British Beef Steak Mince	→ lettuce leaves
→ 1 beaten egg	→ Four white rolls
→ 1 tsp herbs mixed dried	→ 1 sliced beef tomato

Direction

In a deep fryer, heat olive oil, then add onion & cook for 5 mins, or till softened & golden. Set it aside. Mix the herbs, beef mince, and egg inside a mixing bowl. Season with salt and pepper, then stir in the onions. Form four patties with your hands. Heat the burgers approximately 5-6 mins on a heated grill or griddle. Place a piece of cheese over top of the 2nd side to soften slightly as it cooks. Meanwhile, on the BBQ, gently brown the cut-parts of buns. Place the burgers, lettuce, and tomato slices on top. If desired, serve extra ketchup.

BLACKENED SWORDFISH

Prep time: 5mins   **Cook time: 5mins**

Servings: 2

Nutritional information:

Per serving: Kcal 238, Fat: 34g, Carbs: 12g, Protein: 56g

Ingredients	→ 2 tbsp. of Creole seasoning → ¼ cup of melted butter	→ 2 fillets (6 ounce) swordfish fillets

Direction	On moderate flame, warm a casting iron skillet. In a small basin, melt the butter. Put the fish on to a platter after dipping it in butter. Season the fillets with Creole spice and press it in. Put the fish inside the heated pan and cook for 2 minutes, or until it begins to darken but does not burn. Cook for another two min on the 2nd side until charred.

BRAISED SAUCE LAMB WITH OLIVES

Prep time: 30mins   **Cook time: 3hrs**

Servings: 8

Nutritional information:

Per serving: Kcal 444, Fat: 2g, Carbs: 28g, Protein: 7g

Ingredients

→ 2 /3 cup of mild-flavored molasses

→ 8 3/4-pound of lamb shanks

→ 1 cup flour all-purpose

→ 1/3 cup and 2 tbsp. of olive oil

→ 1 1/2 tbsp. of and 1 tsp. of Hungarian sweet paprika

→ 3 large sized onions

→ 1 1/2 cups of white wine dry

→ 1 can (28-ounce) of in juice plum tomatoes, juice reserved, tomatoes crushed

→ 1 1/2 cups of chicken broth low-salt

→ 1/2 cup of fresh chopped Italian parsley and additional

→ Four bay leaves

→ 6 pressed garlic cloves

→ 2 tsp. of lemon peel finely grated

→ 1 lemon, peel and segments cut

→ 3/4 cup of Kalamata olives pitted

Preheat the oven to 350 degrees Fahrenheit. Lay the lamb shanks out on the work surface. To coat the top side, brush 1/2 of the molasses on and season with pepper and salt. In a small mixing bowl, combine flour & 1 1/2 teaspoons paprika. Half of the seasoned flour should be gently sprinkled over the shanks. Repeat with the remaining salt, molasses, pepper, and spiced flour on the other side of the shanks. Inside a heavy big skillet, heat 1/3 cup of oil on moderate flame. In a thin layer, place four lamb shanks. Cook for approximately 8 minutes, turning periodically, until brown color. In a wide roasting pan, place the shanks. Rep with the remaining four shanks in thin layer in the pan. In a large big saucepan, heat the remaining 2 tbsp oil on moderate flame. Toss in the onions. Sauté for approximately 12 minutes, or till deep brown. Bring to one boil, stirring regularly, with the tomatoes, broth, wine, lemon peel, broth, bay leaves, garlic, and the leftover 1 tsp paprika. Bring the mixture to a boil for 5 minutes. Pour the sauce over the shanks in the roasting pan. Shift the shanks gently with tongs to enable the onions & tomatoes to slip beneath. Wrap a layer of parchment paper around the pan, then wrap it securely with foil. Put lamb shanks into the oven & braise until extremely tender, approximately 2 1/4 hours, flipping on each 45 minutes. Place the lamb shanks on baking sheet with a rim. Reserve the roasting pan and pour the pan juices in a heavy big pot. Remove the fat off the top of the pan juices. Cook, stirring often to prevent burning, till sauce is thickened enough to cover a spoon & decreased to seven cups, 18-20 minutes. Combine the lemon segments, olives, and half cup parsley in a mixing bowl. Sprinkle with salt & pepper to taste. Return the lamb shanks to the roasting pan you set aside earlier. Distribute the sauce evenly. Do it ahead of time it's possible to prepare this dish two days ahead of time. Allow 1 hour for cooling. Refrigerate after covering using parchment paper and then foil. Cover and reheat in a 350°F oven for 45 minutes. On a big deep dish, arrange the lamb shanks. Pour the majority of the sauce on top. Add more parsley on top if desired. Serve with the rest of the sauce.

Broccoli Curry Dal

Prep time: 30mins　　　　　**Cook time: 1hr.**

Servings: 4

Nutritional information:

　　　　Per serving: Kcal 445, Fat: 15g, Carbs: 59g, Protein: 25g

Ingredients	
→ 2 medium chopped onions	→ 1 juice of lemon
→ 4 tbsp. of butter or 4 tbsp. of ghee	→ 1 cup of coarsely chopped cashews
→ 1 tsp. of chili powder	→ 2 medium chopped broccolis
→ 2 tsp. of cumin	→ 3 cups of chicken broth
→ 1 1/2 tsp. of black pepper	→ 1/2 cup of dried coconut
→ 1 tsp. of ground coriander	→ 1 tsp. of salt
→ 1 cup of red lentil	→ 1 tbsp. of flour
→ 2 tsp. of turmeric	

Direction

Inside a saucepan, melt the butter, then brown the onions. Chili powder, cumin, pepper, turmeric and coriander are all good additions. 1 minute of stirring and cooking Add the lentils, broth, lemon juice, and if using, the coconut. Boil it, then lower to a low heat and cook for 45 to 55 minutes. 7 minutes of steaming broccoli. Put aside broccoli after submerging it in cold water. Drain 1/3 cup lentil mixture's liquid. To make a smooth paste, mix in the flour. Return to the pan and stir in the broccoli, salt, & nuts, if desired. Cook for five min on low heat. With Basmati rice, serve.

BROCCOLI WITH MULTIPLE VEGGIES

Prep time: 5mins   **Cook time: 40mins**

Servings: 4

Nutritional information:

Per serving: Kcal 231, Fat: 15g, Carbs: 23g, Protein: 8g

Ingredients

- → 1 large chopped zucchini
- → 1 broccoli head, chopped off florets from stalk
- → 2 tsp. of black pepper
- → 1 large chopped yellow squash
- → 3 chopped carrots
- → 1 cup sliced cherry tomatoes
- → 10 ounces of sliced portobello mushrooms
- → 2-3 tsp. of kosher salt
- → ¼ cup olive oil

Direction

Preheat the oven at 425 degrees F. Mix all the veggies with salt, olive oil, and pepper inside a large mixing bowl. Using two jelly roll sheets, divide the veggies. Roast the veggies for 35 to 40 minutes, turning them over after Fifteen minutes to ensure even cooking.

Brussel Sprout and Sheet Pan Chicken

Prep time: 15mins   **Cook time: 20mins**

Servings: 4

Nutritional information:

Per serving: Kcal 351, Fat: 15g, Carbs: 24g, Protein: 28g

Ingredients

→ 2 tbsp. of olive oil, extra-virgin

→ 1 pound of sweet potatoes,

→ ¾ tsp. of salt

→ 3 tbsp. of sherry vinegar

→ 4 cups of Brussels sprouts

→ ¾ tsp. of ground pepper

→ 1 ¼ pounds of skinless, boneless chicken thighs

→ ½ tsp. of dried thyme

→ ½ tsp. of ground cumin

Direction

Preheat the oven at 425 degrees Fahrenheit. Inside a large mixing bowl, mix sweet potatoes using 1 tsp oil & 1/4 tsp salt & pepper. On the rimmed baking sheet, evenly spread. 15 min of roasting in a mixing dish, mix Brussels sprouts using the leftover 1 tbsp oil & 1/4 tsp salt and black pepper. On baking sheet, mix in the sweet potatoes. Cumin, the additional 1/4 tsp salt and black pepper and thyme to season the chicken. Arrange the veggies on top. Roast for another 10-15 minutes, or till the meat is cooked properly and the veggies are soft. Place the chicken on a serving plate and serve. Toss the veggies with the vinegar and serve using the chicken.

CITRUS SCALLOPS AND SHRIMP

Prep time: 20mins   **Cook time: 10mins**

Servings: 4

Nutritional information:

Per serving: Kcal 133, Fat: 1g, Carbs: 7g, Protein: 22g

Ingredients	
→ 12 frozen or fresh large shrimp, deveined and peeled	→ ½ cup of orange juice
→ ½ pound frozen or fresh scallops	→ 1 tsp. of fresh ginger grated
→ 1 tsp. of orange peel finely shredded	→ ⅛ - ¼ tsp. of red pepper ground
→ 2 tbsp. of soy sauce	→ 1 minced clove garlic
→ 1 orange	→ 12 frozen or fresh pea pods

Direction

Any huge scallops should be halved. In a deep dish, place scallops & shrimp inside a plastic container. Combine orange juice, orange peel, ginger, soy sauce, garlic, & red pepper inside a marinade. Pour the sauce over the fish. Close the bag. Refrigerate for 30 minutes after marinating. Drain and set aside the marinade. When using pea pods, simmer for two min in boiling hot water before draining. Alternatively, defrost cold pea pods & drain them. Each shrimp should be wrapped in a pea pod. Pea pods & shrimp alternate among scallops & orange wedges over 4 10-12-inch skewers. About 5 minutes, cook kabobs on a grill immediately on moderate coals. Brush it with marinade after each round. 5–7 minutes longer on the grill, or till shrimp are pink & scallops are opaque. Coat with marinade on a regular basis. This recipe serves 4 people.

CROCKPOT BLACK-EYED SPICY PEAS

Prep time: 30mins   **Cook time: 6hrs**

Servings: 10

Nutritional information:

Per serving: Kcal 199, Fat: 2g, Carbs: 30g, Protein: 15g

Ingredients

→ 1 cube of chicken bouillon

→ 6 cups of water

→ 1 pound of black-eyed peas, dried, sorted & rinsed

→ 2 diced cloves garlic

→ 1 diced onion

→ 1 red diced bell pepper

→ 8 ounces of diced ham

→ 1 jalapeno chili, minced and seeded

→ 1 tsp. of black pepper ground

→ 4 slices of chopped bacon,

→ 1 ½ teaspoons of cumin

→ ½ tsp. of cayenne pepper

→ salt

Direction

Fill a slow cooker halfway with water, then add bouillon cube & stir to dissolve. Toss together the onion, black-eyed peas, bell pepper, garlic, ham, bacon, jalapeno pepper, cumin, cayenne pepper, salt, & pepper in a large mixing bowl. Cook on Slow for six to eight hours, or till the beans become ready, covered in slow cooker.

FILLETS OF BROILED CHICKEN BREASTS & MANGO

Prep time: 5mins   **Cook time: 40mins**

Servings: 6

Nutritional information:

Per serving: Kcal 310, Fat: 4g, Carbs: 33g, Protein: 33g

Ingredients

→ 1/2 tsp of salt	→ 1/2 tsp of black pepper
→ 2 lbs. of skinless, boneless chicken breasts	→ 1 jalapeño diced and seeded
→ 2 tbsp of honey	→ 12 oz of mango chunks frozen or fresh
→ 1 cup of barbecue sauce	

Direction

Preheat the oven to 400 degrees Fahrenheit. Set aside the baking dish that has been sprayed with cooking spray. The jalapeno should be seeded and diced. Season both sides of the chicken breasts using salt and black pepper. Spread 2/3 cup of barbecue sauce over the chicken inside a baking dish. Mango pieces and sliced jalapeno put on top. Drizzle honey on the top, then bake for 40 mins, or till a core temperature of 165°F is reached. Remove the chicken to a large plate and pour the leftover barbecue sauce on it, thickening it with the mangoes, cooking juices, and chilies.

FISH WITH OLIVES, TOMATOES AND CAPERES

Prep time: 10mins   **Cook time: 15mins**

Servings: 4

Nutritional information:

Per serving: Kcal 275, Fat: 10g, Carbs: 8g, Protein: 34g

Ingredients	
→ 250g of cherry tomatoes	→ Four thyme sprigs
→ 4 175g ling fish fillets	→ 2 tbsp drained capers, rinsed
→ 2 cups salad leaves	→ 1-2 tbsp of balsamic vinegar
→ 100g kalamata olives pitted	→ 2 tbsp of olive oil extra virgin

Direction

Preheat oven to 200 degrees Celsius. Sprinkle the olives, tomatoes, thyme sprigs and capers over the fish in your pan, drizzle the olive oil. Bake for about fifteen minutes after seasoning with pepper and salt. Remove the pan from the oven, wrap in foil, and set aside for 5mins to cool. 4 warming plates with the tomatoes, fish, and olives Pour the vinegar on the fish after stirring it in pan juices. Toss fresh salad leaves on the side.

FLORENTINE PORK DUCK

Prep time: 20mins   **Cook time: 70mins**

Servings: 4

Nutritional information:

Per serving: Kcal 284, Fat: 14g, Carbs: 15g, Protein: 23g

Ingredients

→ 2 tbsp fennel seeds

→ 1.2kg on the bone pork loin

→ 4 peeled apples

→ 2 tsp of salt

→ 80ml of olive oil extra virgin

→ 1 tsp of black pepper

→ 100ml white wine

Direction

Take the bones out from pork loin with a sharp knife, but just don't discard them. Fennel seeds, salt and black pepper, are crushed together and massaged into the meat. Reposition the loin on bones and secure it with butcher's thread. Wrap with plastic wrap and place in the refrigerator overnight. Take the meat out from your fridge approximately 40 mins before you want to cook this to get it down to room temperature. Preheat oven at 180°C on the oven dial. Drizzle the olive oil over the meat inside a deep pan. Cook meat for around 40 minutes. Spoon over the wine and place the apple all around the meat when it becomes crisp & golden. Using salt and black pepper, sprinkle the apples. Raise the cooking temperature to 200°C gas 6 and continue to cook pork loin for yet another 40 minutes, basting it with pan juices as needed. Cover the meat using aluminum foil. Before slicing, take the pork loin out from oven, cover it in foil, and let it sit for 30 minutes. Serve with cooked apples & pan juices poured on top.

Green Olives With Lemon Mutton

Prep time: 15mins   **Cook time: 13,1/2hrs.**

Servings: 8

Nutritional information:

Per serving: Kcal 738, Fat: 57g, Carbs: 13g, Protein: 43g

Ingredients

- → 5 minced garlic cloves
- → 1/4 cup olive oil extra-virgin
- → Two strips (2 1/2-inch) of lemon zest
- → 2 tsp. of sweet paprika
- → 2 tsp. of ground ginger
- → 2 tsp. of ground coriander
- → 1 tsp. of black pepper freshly ground
- → 1 tsp. of ground cumin
- → 1/4 tsp. of cayenne pepper
- → Pinch saffron threads
- → 1/4 tsp. of ground cloves

- → Kosher salt
- → 1 3-inch of cinnamon stick
- → 3 1/2 pounds lamb shoulder, boneless
- → 6 large thinly sliced carrots,
- → 1 onion
- → 3 tbsp. of fresh lemon juice
- → 4 cups of water
- → 1 cup parsley, flat-leaf chopped
- → 2 cups green Picholine olives, pitted, rinsed
- → 1 cup of chopped cilantro leaves

Direction

Mix the garlic, olive oil, lemon zest, paprika, ginger, coriander, black pepper, cumin, cayenne, saffron, cloves, cinnamon stick, & 1 tbsp kosher salt together in a large mixing basin. Toss in the lamb and coat it. Refrigerate about 4-6 hours before serving. Remove the lemon zest, then scrape the meat and spices in medium enameled cast-iron pan. Bring the carrots, water, and onion to a low simmer. Cover and simmer over low heat for 2 hours, or till the lamb seems to be very soft. Remove any excess from the soup using a spoon. Heat for 2 mins after adding the olives & seasoning with salt. Mix in the cilantro, parsley, and lemon juice after removing the pan from heat. Into bowls, ladle the soup and serve.

Italian Poached Scallops

Prep time: 20mins **Cook time: 10mins**

Servings: 4

Nutritional information:

Per serving: Kcal 227, Fat: 11g, Carbs: 17g, Protein: 16g

Ingredients

→ 4 carrots

→ 2 tbsp. of olive oil

→ 2 leeks thinly sliced

→ 2 tbsp. of finely chopped pine nuts

→ 12 large sized sea scallops

→ ½ cup of white wine dry

→ Kosher salt & black pepper

→ 1 finely chopped clove garlic

→ 1 cup parsley, fresh finely chopped, flat-leaf

Direction

In a medium saucepan, heat 1 tbsp of the oil on moderate flame. Cook, stirring occasionally, for 2 minutes after adding the carrots & leeks. Bring wine & half cup of water to a boil. Put the scallops over top of the veggies, then season with 1/2 tsp salt & 1/4 tsp pepper. Lower heat to medium-low & cook, covered, for approximately 8 minutes, just until the scallop is opaque through. Place the scallops on a serving platter. Mix the pine nuts, garlic, parsley, and the additional tablespoon oil in a mixing bowl. Garnish the scallops with a sauce made from the veggies and broth. Instead of cutting the garlic, parsley, & pine nuts using hand, mix them with 1 tbsp of olive oil inside a food processor.

Lamb & Coconut

Prep time: 5mins   **Cook time: 30mins**

Servings: 4

Nutritional information:

Per serving: Kcal 506, Fat: 40g, Carbs: 8g, Protein: 28g

Ingredients

→ 1 medium coarsely chopped onion

→ 2 tablespoons of vegetable oil

→ 2 minced garlic cloves

→ 1 1/2 pounds of lean lamb ground

→ 1 tablespoon fresh ginger minced

→ 1 1/2 tablespoons of curry powder

→ Hot sauce

→ One can (14-ounce) of coconut milk, unsweetened, stirred

→ 1 medium peeled sweet potato

→ Salt and ground pepper

→ 1 cup low-sodium chicken stock

→ 1/3 cup cilantro coarsely chopped

→ 1/2 cup of frozen thawed baby peas

Direction

Heat oil in a big, deep skillet till it shimmers. Cook, stirring occasionally, until the garlic, onion, and ginger are slightly cooked approximately 4 minutes. Heat, splitting up the lamb using wooden spoon, on medium heat till it begins to brown, approximately 10 minutes. Cook for an additional minutes after adding the curry powder & sweet potato. Sprinkle pepper and salt after adding coconut milk & stock. Cover slightly and cook over medium heat for approximately 15 minutes, just until sweet potato is cooked. Cook till the peas are cooked thoroughly. Serve with spicy sauce & cilantro on the side.

LIGHTLY BREADED GRILLED CHICKEN

Prep time: 10mins   **Cook time: 6mins**

Servings: 4

Nutritional information:

Per serving: Kcal 327, Fat: 11g, Carbs: 11g, Protein: 42g

Ingredients

→ 1 teaspoon dried chives minced

→ 1 teaspoon of dried thyme

→ 1/2 teaspoon of dried basil

→ 1/4 cup Parmesan cheese grated

→ 1 large beaten egg

→ 1/2 cup breadcrumbs

→ 1/2 teaspoon of kosher salt

→ 1 tablespoon of olive oil

→ 1/8 teaspoon black pepper freshly ground

→ 4 skinless, boneless chicken breasts

Direction

Collect the necessary components. Prepare a two-sided grill or a pan with two sides. Combine the chives, thyme, basil, Parmesan, breadcrumbs, and salt & pepper in a small pan. Pour the oil on the crumbs and gently massage it in until they are evenly covered. Place the chicken breasts between two waxed sheets. Lightly press the breasts with a rolling pin till they are approximately 1/2-inch thickness. Chicken breasts should be dipped in beaten egg. Next, pressing firmly into mixture of breadcrumbs, coat every egg-coated breast completely with crumbs. Heat chicken breasts approximately 4-6 minutes on your grill until cooked properly to 160 F & juices flow clear. Serve right away.

Linguine and Mixed Seafood

Prep time: 5mins   **Cook time: 15mins**

Servings: 4

Nutritional information:

Per serving: Kcal 164, Fat: 7g, Carbs: 8g, Protein: 8g

Ingredients

→ 2 tbsp of olive oil	→ 1 lemon
→ 400g spaghetti or linguine	→ 200g of seafood selection
→ 2 thinly sliced garlic cloves	→ 220g of cherry tomatoes
→ 200ml white wine dry	→ handful roughly chopped fresh parsley
→ ½ finely chopped and deseeded red chili	

Direction

Bring the large pot of water which is salted to a boil, then add the pasta & cook as per the package directions. Next, in a big frying pan on moderate heat, heat the oil. Cook about 30 seconds to 1 minute, until garlic & chili are just starting to turn golden. Put in the wine and let to bubble until it has been reduced by 1/2. To tender the tomatoes, toss them into your pan and heat for 1-2 minutes. Cook for another 1-2 minutes, or until seafood mixture is thoroughly heated. Rinse cooked pasta and set aside approximately a cup cooking water. Add the seafood & tomato mixture into the pasta inside the empty pan. =To loosen, put a bit of pasta boiling water, and toss together everything till thoroughly combined, add water as required. Distribute among serving plates and top with chopped parsley. Garnish with a slice of lemon over the top.

MEDITERRANEAN BREAST CHICKEN & AVOCADO TAPENAD

Prep time: 5mins   **Cook time: 10mins**

Servings: 4

Nutritional information:

Per serving: Kcal 277, Fat: 16g, Carbs: 7g, Protein: 26g

Ingredients

→ 4 skinless boneless chicken breasts

→ 1 tablespoon lemon peel grated

→ 5 tablespoons lemon juice, fresh

→ 2 tablespoons of olive oil

→ 1 teaspoon of olive oil

→ 1 finely chopped garlic clove

→ 1/2 teaspoon of salt

→ 1/4 teaspoon black pepper

→ 2 tablespoons finely sliced basil leaves

→ 2 mashed and roasted garlic cloves

→ 1/2 teaspoon of sea salt

→ 1/4 teaspoon ground pepper

→ 1 large finely chopped, ripe Hass avocado

→ 3 tablespoons rinsed capers

→ 1 medium finely chopped and seeded tomatoes

→ 1/4 cup thinly sliced olive stuffed with green pimento

Direction

Combine chicken, 2 tbsp lemon juice, lemon peel, garlic, 2 tbsp olive oil, salt, & pepper in a sealed container plastic bag. Chill for thirty min after sealing the bag. Combine the leftover 3 tbsp lemon juice, 1/2 tsp olive oil, roasted garlic, sea salt, and freshly pepper in a mixing bowl. Set aside the green olives, tomato, capers, avocado and basil. Remove the chicken from the bag and toss out the marinade. Cook for 4-5 minutes each side over moderate coals, or until required level of doneness is reached. Avocado Tapenade is a great addition to this dish.

Mushrooms and Olives Braised Pork

Prep time: 40mins   **Cook time: 5hrs**

Servings: 6

Nutritional information:

Per serving: Kcal 404, Fat: 33g, Carbs: 5g, Protein: 21g

Ingredients	
→ 45 ml olive oil (3 tbsp)	→ Salt & pepper
→ 1 pork shoulder, roast (4 lb) 1.8 kg with bone	→ 125 ml white wine (1/2 cup)
→ 2 chopped onions	→ 30 ml unbleached flour (2 tbsp) all-purpose
→ 2 chopped cloves garlic	→ 1 can diced tomatoes (14 oz/398 ml)
→ 2 diced and seeded red bell peppers	
→ 225 g white mushrooms (1/2 lb.)	→ 500 ml chicken broth (2 cups)

Direction

Preheat oven to 350°F with the wire shelf in place. Cook the pork in 30 ml oil in a pan oven - safe. Salt & pepper to taste. Place the meat on a platter and set it aside. Brown the veggies in the residual oil in the very same pan. Toss with in flour and fully combine. With wine, deglaze pan. Toss in the tomatoes & broth. Bring to the boil while continually whisking. Toss the meat back into the pan. Cover and cook for approximately three hours in oven. And during cooking process, turn your meat 2-3 times. Uncover. Cook for 1 hour more, just until the pork is fork soft. Garnish with some mashed potatoes if preferred.

PASTA WITH MULTIPLE VEGGIES

Prep time: 20mins   **Cook time: 40mins**

Servings: 10

Nutritional information:

Per serving: Kcal 522, Fat: 31g, Carbs: 42g, Protein: 19g

Ingredients

→ 2 tablespoons of olive oil

→ 1 pound of penne pasta

→ ½ pound trimmed asparagus

→ 1 cup red bell pepper chopped

→ 1 cup broccoli florets

→ 1 cup zucchini chopped

→ 2 tablespoons of minced garlic

→ 8 ounces Parmesan cheese grated

→ ¾ cup of butter

→ 2 cups of tomatoes, sun-dried

→ 5 ounces diced prosciutto

Direction

Preheat the oven to 375° Fahrenheit. A big saucepan of salted boiling water should be brought to a boil. Heat for 8-10 minutes, or till pasta is al dente; drain. Toss with a little olive oil. Roast asparagus, bell pepper, broccoli, and zucchini inside a large pan on moderate heat till dark brown flecks appear. Remove from the equation. Melt butter inside a large pan on moderate heat. Garlic, prosciutto & sun-dried tomatoes in a skillet until cooked completely. Toss penne in roasted veggies and Parmesan cheese. Fill baking dish with the mixture. Preheat the oven to 350°F and bake for 3-40 mins, or until hot.

Mutton Salad with Greek Dressing

Prep time:4hrs 15mins   **Cook time: 10mins**

Servings: 4

Nutritional information:

Per serving: Kcal 554, Fat: 36g, Carbs: 30g, Protein: 30g

Ingredients

→ 2 tbsp olive oil, extra virgin

→ 60ml red wine (1/4 cup)

→ 2 bay leaves, torn, fresh

→ 2 smashed garlic cloves

→ 2 tsp thyme leaves chopped

→ 500g of lamb backstraps

→ Black olive tapenade

→ Four thick slices crusty bread

→ 1 baby leaves separated cos lettuce

→ 1 thinly sliced red onion

→ 300g coarsely crumbled block feta

→ 4 thinly sliced qukes (baby cucumbers)

→ 1 finely chopped garlic clove

→ Oregano sprigs

→ Cherry truss tomatoes

→ Lemon & garlic dressing

→ 2 tbsp lemon juice

→ 80ml olive oil extra virgin (1/3 cup)

Direction

In a ceramic or glass bowl, mix the wine, bay leaves, olive oil, garlic and thyme. Season with salt and pepper. Turn your lamb to cover it in the sauce. Cover, then marinate for four hours inside the refrigerator. Inside a screw-top jar, combine all of the components for dressing. Season. To blend, seal the container and shake it vigorously. Set it aside to allow the flavors to meld. Preheat a chargrill pan to high heat. Take the lamb out from marinade and blot it dry with paper towels. For moderate, cook approximately 3-4 mins, or until done to your preference. Allow for a five - minute rest period. Cut the lamb into slices. Meanwhile, brush the bread with more oil and brown it on your grill or even in a pan for chargrill for 1-2 mins. Remove the tapenade and distribute it on top. On a serving tray, arrange the bread, lamb, feta, lettuce, onion, tomatoes and cucumber. Sprinkle with some more oil and oregano, if desired. Eat with dressing on the side.

PORK BRUSCHETTA

Prep time: 5mins   **Cook time: 25mins**

Servings: 2

Nutritional information:

Per serving: Kcal 340, Fat: 13g, Carbs: 15g, Protein: 31g

Ingredients

→ 2 Tbsp. Pork Seasoned Coating Mix

→ 2 butterflied pork chops boneless (1/2 lb.)

→ 1/2 cup Mozzarella Cheese, Part-Skim Low-Moisture Shredded

→ 1/4 cup of Tomato Vinaigrette Dressing Sun-Dried

→ 1 chopped plum tomato

Direction

Preheat the oven to 425 degrees Fahrenheit. Coat the chops in the coating mix according to the package directions. Place on your baking sheet that has been coated with nonstick cooking spray. Bake for 20 minutes, or till chops are cooked through (160°F). Meanwhile, put the tomatoes and the dressing in a mixing bowl. Chops should be topped with the tomato mixture & cheese. Bake for 5 minutes, or till cheese is completely melted.

PORK FROM THE MEDITERRANEAN

Prep time: 10mins **Cook time: 35mins**

Servings: 4

Nutritional information:

Per serving: Kcal 161, Fat: 5g, Carbs: 1g, Protein: 25g

Ingredients

→ ¼ teaspoon of salt

→ 3 minced cloves garlic

→ 4 bone-in or boneless pork loin chops

→ 1 tablespoon fresh rosemary, finely snipped or 1 tsp. of crushed dried rosemary

→ ¼ teaspoon black pepper freshly ground

Direction

Preheat the oven to 425 ° F. Line a small roasting pan using foil if preferred. Season the chops on both sides with pepper and salt and put aside. Mix rosemary & garlic inside a small bowl. Apply rosemary mixture to all edges of the chops and massage it in using your fingertips. In a small roasting pan, arrange the chops on the rack. Chops should be roasted for ten min. Reduce the oven temperature to 350°F and keep roasting for another 25 mins, or till no pinkish color remains (160°F) and the juices flow clear.

Rigatoni & Minced Chicken

Prep time: 5mins   **Cook time: 15mins**

Servings: 4

Nutritional information:

Per serving: Kcal 398, Fat: 11g, Carbs: 50g, Protein: 23g

Ingredients

→ 1 lb. of ground chicken

→ 3 minced garlic cloves

→ 1 can (5.5 oz) of tomato paste

→ 12 oz of rigatoni pasta or penne pasta

→ 1 ½ cups of frozen peas

→ 1 can of crushed tomatoes

→ 1 tsp of dried basil

→ ¼ tsp of red pepper flakes

→ ½ cup feta cheese crumbled

Direction

Cook pasta as per package directions in a saucepan of boiling water. Drain the spaghetti and rinse it under cool water. Set it aside. 1 tbsp of cooking oil and minced garlic, 60 seconds in a cooking pot on medium flame. Combine the ground chicken & stir well. Cook until the chicken has lost its pink color. Add tomato paste and mix well. In a large skillet, combine the peas, cooked pasta, dried basil, smashed tomatoes, & red pepper flakes. Combine all of the ingredients in a pot and cook for 10 minutes. Remove from the pan and top some feta cheese crumbles. Serve by scooping into plates.

Salad of Warm Lamb and Avocado

Servings: 4

Nutritional information:

Per serving: Kcal 924, Fat: 69g, Carbs: 23g, Protein: 51g

Ingredients	
→ 1/4 cup olive oil extra virgin	→ 1/2 cup green olives pitted(75g)
→ 800g of lamb steaks	→ 1 large sliced, peeled ripe avocado
→ 600g of drained, chat potatoes	→ 4 cups watercress sprigs
→ 200g of basil pesto	

Direction

Preheat a char-grill plate or a barbeque to moderate heat. Gently pound the lambs with a steak mallet to compress it slightly, and brush with 1 tbsp oil. Cook the lamb about 1 to 2 minutes on every surface or until it reaches your desired doneness. Add salt &pepper to taste, then put aside. Slice potatoes, then combine with avocado, watercress, olives, the leftover oil and pesto inside a large mixing bowl. Season with salt and pepper to taste. Gently blend the ingredients with your hands. Serve the lamb & potato combination on individual plates. Serve.

Spicy Rigatoni With Mussels

Prep time: 5mins **Cook time: 25mins**

Servings: 4

Nutritional information:

Per serving: Kcal 419, Fat: 11g, Carbs: 54g, Protein: 2g

Ingredients

→ 2 tablespoons of olive oil

→ ½ lb. fettuccine, spaghetti, pasta, or linguine

→ ½ cup finely diced onion

→ 1 lb. fresh debearded and scrubbed live mussels

→ 1 tablespoon minced garlic

→ 1 tablespoon chopped fresh parsley 2 tablespoons of cooking wine

→ ½ teaspoon of salt

→ 1 can tomato sauce

→ ½ teaspoon of black pepper

→ 1 tablespoon of freshly grated Parmesan cheese,

→ 1 cup of cherry tomatoes

Direction

Over moderate flame, boil a big pot of water with salt. Cook for 8 to 10 minutes, or as per package guidelines, till spaghetti noodles are al dente. Drain the water well and leave it aside. Meanwhile, in a wide saucepan or big skillet, heat the oil on moderate flame for two min, or until it is boiling hot & shimmering. Sauté the garlic and onions until aromatic and tender, about 2-3 minutes. Toss in the mussels and the wine. Steam about 6 to 8 minutes, covered, till all the shells are fully open. And if you do not have a lid, turn the mussels regularly to ensure equal cooking. Reduce heat to medium-low and stir in the tomato sauce & pasta. Toss very well to combine, then reduce to a low heat for 3-5 mins to bring your sauce to simmer. Salt and black pepper to taste after adding the cherry tomatoes. Serve warm with parmesan & parsley over top.

Spicy Stuffed Tilapia

Prep time: 20mins   **Cook time: 25mins**

Servings: 4

Nutritional information:

Per serving: Kcal 608, Fat: 47g, Carbs: 9g, Protein: 40g

Ingredients

- → 1 finely chopped celery rib
- → 1 small finely chopped onion
- → 1/4 cup butter
- → 1/3 cup bread crumbs dry
- → 1/4 teaspoon of paprika
- → 1 cup drained lump crabmeat
- → 1/3 cup of mayonnaise
- → 2 tablespoons drained diced pimientos
- → 1 large beaten egg
- → 1/4 teaspoon of seafood seasoning
- → 1/4 teaspoon of salt
- → 4 tilapia fillets

Direction

Cook onion & celery in quarter cup butter inside a large pan until soft. Take the heat off and combine the crab, mayonnaise, bread crumbs, egg, seafood spice and pimientos in a mixing bowl. Cover the fillets with 1/3 cup of crab mixture. Roll each one up starting at the pointed end and fasten with toothpicks. Inside a greased 9-inch square baking sheet, place the seam side downwards. Remaining butter should be melted and drizzled over the fish. Season with paprika & salt. Bake, and uncover, at 400° about 25-thirty min, or till fish starts to flake readily using a fork. Toothpicks should be discarded. Pour the pan juices on the fish.

STEW WITH BEEF

Prep time: 20mins   **Cook time: 12hrs**

Servings: 6

Nutritional information:

Per serving: Kcal 576, Fat: 30g, Carbs: 29g, Protein: 44g

Ingredients

→ ¼ cup flour all-purpose

→ 2 pounds of beef stew meat

→ ½ teaspoon of salt

→ 1 minced clove garlic

→ ½ teaspoon of black pepper

→ One bay leaf

→ 1 teaspoon of Worcestershire sauce

→ 1 teaspoon of paprika

→ 1 stalk chopped celery

→ 1 chopped onion

→ 3 diced potatoes

→ 1 ½ cups of beef broth

→ 4 sliced carrots

Direction

Inside a slow cooker, place the meat. Combine the salt, flour, and pepper inside a small basin; pour on the meat, then swirl to coat this with flour mixture. Add the bay leaf, garlic, paprika, onion, Worcestershire sauce, beef broth, carrots, potatoes, and celery into the saucepan and stir to combine. Cook over low for 10-12 hrs. Or maximum for 4-6 hours, covered.

Stuffed Sesame Chicken Breasts

Prep time: 10mins   **Cook time: 15mins**

Servings: 4

Nutritional information:

Per serving: Kcal 509, Fat: 28g, Carbs: 23g, Protein: 41g

Ingredients

→ 4 6-ounce chicken-breast boneless halves

→ 1 cup white rice long-grain

→ 2 tablespoons of grated ginger

→ 2 bunches of spinach trimmed

→ 1 tablespoon of olive oil

→ kosher salt & pepper

→ 2 tablespoons of sesame oil

Direction

Follow the package instructions for cooking the rice. In the meanwhile, dry chicken using paper towels. Place the ginger beneath the skin with care. 1 tsp and 1/4 tsp pepper, to taste. In a big skillet, heat olive oil on moderate flame. Cook chicken, skin-side downwards, for 7 minutes, or till the skin becomes crisp. Cook, covered, till the meat is cooked through, approximately 6 minutes. In a separate big skillet, heat sesame oil & seeds on moderate flame till the seeds turn light gold, approximately 2 minutes. Cook till the spinach has wilted, adding 1/2 tbsp & 1/8 tsp pepper. Serve it with the rice and chicken on top of the salad.

TROUT AND BLACK OLIVES

Prep time: 5mins   **Cook time: 15mins**

Servings: 4

Nutritional information:

Per serving: Kcal 215, Fat: 8g, Carbs: 3g, Protein: 33g

Ingredients	
→ ¼ cup pitted manzanilla coarsely chopped	→ ¼ teaspoon garlic minced
→ 1 cup tomato finely chopped	→ 4 trout fillets (6-ounce)
→ 1 teaspoon olive oil extra-virgin	→ ½ teaspoon of salt
→ ¼ teaspoon black pepper freshly ground	→ 2 tablespoons fresh parsley minced
→ Cooking spray	

Direction

Preheat the oven to 400 degrees Fahrenheit. In a smaller mixing dish, combine the first five ingredients. Prepare a baking sheet by lining it with foil and spraying it using cooking spray. Place the fish, skin edge down, on the baking sheet that has been prepared. Parsley, pepper and salt should be uniformly distributed. Preheat oven to 400°F and bake approximately 8 mins, or till salmon flakes readily when checked using a fork, or till desired doneness is reached. Serve with the olive mixture on the side.

LENTIL VEGAN BURGERS

Prep time: 15mins   **Cook time: 55mins**

Servings: 9

Nutritional information:

Per serving: Kcal 174, Fat: 3g, Carbs: 28g, Protein: 9g

Ingredients		
→ 2 1/2 cups of water	→ 3/4 cup of breadcrumbs
→ 1 cup well rinsed dry lentils,	→ 1 diced carrot
	→ 1 tablespoon of soy sauce
→ 1/2 teaspoon of salt	
→ 1/2 medium diced onion	→ 1 teaspoon of pepper
	→ 3/4 cup finely ground rolled oats
→ 1 tablespoon of olive oil	

Direction

Lentils should be cooked for 45 min in salted water. . In a little amount of oil, fry onions & carrots until tender, approximately 5 minutes. Combine the prepared ingredients, soy sauce, pepper, oats, & bread crumbs in a mixing bowl. Form your mixture in the patties when it is heated; it will create 8-10 burgers. After that, the burgers may be lightly fried for 1 to 2 mins on every side and baked for fifteen min at 200°C.

WATERCREES & PEPPER

Prep time: 15mins   **Cook time: 15mins**

Servings: 4

Nutritional information:

Per serving: Kcal 218, Fat: 13g, Carbs: 6g, Protein: 17g

Ingredients	
→ 1 tablespoon of olive oil	→ 1 yellow thinly sliced bell pepper
→ 2 cloves sliced garlic,	→ 8 ounces trimmed watercress
→ ¼ teaspoon red pepper crushed	→ ¼ cup red onion thinly sliced

Direction

Cook garlic with oil inside a large pan on moderate heat, turning often, till fragrant, about 1 minute. Cook, turning often until the bell pepper & onion are softened, approximately 3 minutes. Season with salt and pepper, then heat until the watercress wilts, approximately 2 minutes.

5.4 Salads

Apple Salad with Bok Choy

Prep time: 20mins   **Cook time: 0mins**

Servings: 8

Nutritional information:

Per serving: Kcal 65, Fat: 3g, Carbs: 8g, Protein: 1.5g

Ingredients

→ ⅓ cup mayonnaise reduced-fat

→ ⅓ cup sour cream reduced-fat

→ 2 tablespoons of vinegar white-wine

→ ½ teaspoon of celery salt

→ 2 teaspoons of sugar

→ ½ cup red onion

→ ¼ teaspoon of salt

→ 1 large apple

→ 6 cups bok choy

→ 1 large shredded carrot

Direction

Take a large mixing bowl, whisk together mayonnaise, sour cream, vinegar, celery salt, sugar (you can also use honey), and salt until smooth. Toss in the apple, bok choy, carrots, and onion to coat.

Brussels Sprouts & Shredded Salad

Prep time: 20mins   **Cook time: 0mins**

Servings: 8

Nutritional information:

Per serving: Kcal 230, Fat: 14g, Carbs: 22g, Protein: 6g

Ingredients

→ ¼ cup of cider vinegar

→ 1 shallot

→ ¼ cup of sunflower oil

→ ½ teaspoon of honey

→ 2 tablespoons of Dijon mustard

→ ½ teaspoon of salt

→ 6 cups of Brussels sprouts

→ ¼ teaspoon black pepper

→ ⅓ cup pumpkin seeds

→ 2 apples

→ ⅓ cup almonds

→ ½ cup cranberries

→ ⅓ cup sunflower kernels

Direction

In a mixing bowl, combine the vinegar, shallot, oil, honey, Dijon mustard, pepper & salt. Toss Brussels sprouts, cranberries, apples, almonds, pumpkin seeds & sunflower seeds together in a dish with the vinegar mixture.

DETOX THAI TOFU SALAD

Prep time: 15mins **Cook time: 2mins**

Servings: 4

Nutritional information:

Per serving: Kcal 145, Fat: 9g, Carbs: 10g, Protein: 8g

Ingredients

→ ½ teaspoon ginger root

→ 1 tablespoon chili sauce

→ 2 cloves of garlic

→ 1 tablespoon of sesame oil

→ 1 tablespoon soy sauce

→ 2 tablespoons peanuts

→ ½ package tofu

→ 2 carrots

→ 1 cup of snow peas

→ 1 cup red cabbage

Direction

Combine the ginger, chilli sauce, garlic, sesame oil & soy sauce in a big mixing bowl. Place the tofu in the marinade and marinate in your refrigerator for about 1 hour. A pot having water should be brought to the boil. Cook your snow peas for 1- 2 minutes, then place them in a container having cold water to cool. Drain the water and put it aside. To serve, toss together the carrots, peas, cabbage, peanuts & the tofu, then marinade.

DIJON VINAIGRETTE ASPARAGUS

Prep time: 17mins   **Cook time: 3mins**

Servings: 4

Nutritional information:

Per serving: Kcal 57, Fat: 3g, Carbs: 5g, Protein: 2.5g

Ingredients	
→ 1 1/2 tbsp of red wine vinegar	→ 1 tbsp olive oil
→ 1 pound of asparagus	→ kosher salt & pepper
→ 1 tsp of Dijon Mustard	→ 2 tsp parsley

Direction

Whisk together mustard, vinegar, & 1 tablespoon oil in a mixing bowl. Season with pepper & salt also adds some parsley. For about 2 to 3 minutes, boil or steam asparagus until tender & cooked. To stop its cooking, drain & then rinse under water. Drizzle the vinaigrette over the asparagus in a serving dish. It may be served hot or cold, as you wish.

ORANGE – SESAME SALAD

Prep time: 10mins   **Cook time: 0mins**

Servings: 4

Nutritional information:

Per serving: Kcal 136, Fat: 11g, Carbs: 7g, Protein: 1g

Ingredients	
→ 3 oranges	→ 2 tsp of sesame oil
→ 1 bag salad leaves	→ 1/4 cup of olive oil
→ 1 cucumber	→ 2 tsp of balsamic vinegar
→ Salt & pepper	

Direction

In a mixing bowl, add the salad leaves. Cucumbers should be halved lengthwise and finely sliced diagonally. Toss in with salad leaves. Remove the top and bottom of each orange. In a clockwise manner, cut its skin away, just going to delve enough in order to remove the white pith & the skin. To split the segments, slice between the flesh & the membrane. In a jug, combine the oils & vinegar. Season with pepper & salt. Toss the salad in the dressing to mix.

Roasted Beets and Asparagus Salad With Black Cherry Vinaigrette

Prep time: 20mins   **Cook time: 45mins**

Servings: 4

Nutritional information:

Per serving: Kcal 410, Fat: 27g, Carbs: 42g, Protein: 5g

Ingredients

- → olive oil
- → 2 pounds beets
- → Kosher salt & black pepper
- → 2 tablespoons of balsamic vinegar
- → 1/4 cup cherries
- → 1 teaspoon of sherry vinegar
- → Kosher salt & black pepper
- → 2 tablespoons fresh mint
- → 1/2 cup olive oil
- → 1 cup kale leaves
- → 1/3 cup goat cheese
- → 2 tablespoons of pepitas

Direction

Preheat oven to around 400 degrees Fahrenheit. Place a big piece of foil on the top of your roasting dish & equally distribute the beets over it. Season with salt & pepper and a drizzle of olive oil. Cover with a second piece of foil & crimp the edges to seal them. Make holes on the top to let the steam out. Roast in an oven for about 30-45 minutes or until your beets are soft. Remove it from an oven. Leave to cool inside the foil bag before removing and discarding the skins. Take a large mixing bowl, quarter your peeled beets then place in it. Drain and roughly slice the cherries. While whisking together the cherries & vinegars, drizzle some olive oil gently until it softly dissolves. Add s alt & pepper to taste. Keep it aside until you're ready to utilize it. Combine the hot beets and your prepared cherry vinaigrette in a mixing bowl. Toss in the pepitas, kale, goat cheese, & mint until well combined. Sprinkle salt & pepper to taste.

Quinoa Mango salad

Prep time: 30mins   **Cook time: 12mins**

Servings: 12

Nutritional information:

Per serving: Kcal 126, Fat: 5g, Carbs: 17g, Protein: 2g

Ingredients	
→ 1 teaspoon of salt	→ ¼ cup Corn Oil
→ 2 cups of water	→ 1 tablespoon of mango chutney
→ 1 cup of quinoa	→ 2 tablespoons of white wine vinegar
→ 1 cup cucumber	
→ 3 mangoes	→ ¼ teaspoon Ginger
→ ½ cup red bell pepper	→ ¼ teaspoon Black Pepper
→ 2 cups baby spinach	→ ¼ teaspoon Mustard
→ ⅓ cup green onions	→ 1 ½ teaspoons Curry Powder

Direction

Take a medium sized pan bring the salt & water to a boil. Cook, stirring occasionally until quinoa is cooked but still solid to the bite, approximately 12 minutes of time. Remove from the flame and set aside for about 5 minutes to cool. Put in a medium mixing bowl. Toss quinoa with mango, red pepper, cucumber, & onion. Mix thoroughly. To prepare the dressing, take a food processor, combine the oil, vinegar, oil, chutney, curry, black pepper, mustard, & ginger in it, blend well. Toss the quinoa mixture with 1/4 cup of your dressing. Mix to coat well. Place salad of quinoa on the top of spinach or combine spinach and quinoa salad. Drizzle the rest of your dressing on top. If desired, chill.

Salad of Couscous With Spicy Citrus Dressing

Prep time: 20mins   **Cook time: 5mins**

Servings: 10

Nutritional information:

Per serving: Kcal 156, Fat: 3g, Carbs: 28g, Protein: 6g

Ingredients

→ 3 tablespoons of lime juice

→ ¼ cup fresh cilantro

→ 2 tablespoons of canola oil

→ ⅛ teaspoon of salt

→ 1 ½ teaspoons ginger

→ ⅛ teaspoon of cayenne pepper

→ 1 cup couscous

→ ¼ cup scallions

→ 1 ¼ cups of water

→ 1 can of black beans

→ 1 red bell pepper

→ 2 cups spinach

→ 1 mango

Direction

To make the dressing, combine lime juice, cilantro, oil, ginger, cayenne pepper & salt in a mixing bowl. Leave aside. In a frying pan, bring 1-1/4 cup water to a boil. Remove the pan from the heat. Cover & let aside for about 5 minutes after adding the couscous. Using a fork, fluff your mixture. Allow it to cool for approximately 10 minutes at room temperature. In a mixing bowl, combine the spinach, beans, bell pepper, scallions & mango. Toss in the couscous and the leftover dressing. Toss to evenly coat. Serve right once, or wrap it with foil, then refrigerate for about 24 hours in your refrigerator.

Salad of Lettuce Leaf and Balsamic Vinaigrette with Carrots

Prep time: 20mins   **Cook time: 0mins**

Servings: 6

Nutritional information:

Per serving: Kcal 228, Fat: 19g, Carbs: 12g, Protein: 3g

Ingredients

- → ½ bunch spinach
- → ½ bunch of kale
- → ½ head of romaine lettuce
- → 1 cucumber, diced
- → 1 carrot
- → ½ red bell pepper
- → ½ cup olive oil
- → ½ cup of balsamic vinegar
- → 1 pinch of lemon pepper
- → 1 tablespoon of lemon juice
- → 1 pinch black pepper
- → 1 pinch of sea salt
- → 1 pinch of garlic powder

Direction

Inside a large bowl, combine the spinach, kale, lettuce, cucumber, carrot, & red bell-pepper. In an air-tight container with a lid, combine olive oil, balsamic vinegar, lemon juice, pepper, sea salt, garlic powder, & lemon pepper in it, close and shake until well combined. Toss your salad while pour dressing to coat it.

Salad of Marinated Mushrooms

Prep time: 10mins   **Cook time: 0mins**

Servings: 4

Nutritional information:

Per serving: Kcal 107, Fat: 7g, Carbs: 9g, Protein: 4g

Ingredients	
→ 2 tablespoons of olive oil	→ 1 pound of mushrooms
→ ¼ cup balsamic vinegar	→ salt and black pepper
→ 1 clove of garlic	→ 1 sweet onion
→ 2 tablespoons parsley	

Direction

Inside a small mixing bowl, combine olive oil, balsamic vinegar, garlic, pepper & salt in it. Combine the mushrooms and onion in a mixing bowl of large size. Pour the balsamic vinegar mixture over the top and whisk gently until everything is completely mixed. Cover and marinate for about 6-8 hours in your refrigerator, stirring either once or twice during that period. Well before serving, garnish with some parsley.

Salad of Mixed Greens & Strawberry

Prep time: 15mins   **Cook time: 0mins**

Servings: 4

Nutritional information:

Per serving: Kcal 179, Fat: 8g, Carbs: 10g, Protein: 5g

Ingredients	
→ 1 cup strawberries	→ 2 tablespoons of canola oil
→ 1 package salad greens	→ 2 tablespoons of sugar
→ 2 tablespoons almonds	→ 1/4 teaspoon of salt
→ 1/4 teaspoon mustard	→ 4 teaspoons of red wine vinegar

Direction

Inside a large mixing bowl, combine the salad leaves, almonds & strawberries. In another mixing bowl, whisk together the dressing ingredients, pour over the mixture of salad and toss to combine.

Salad of Raspberries & Leaf Lettuce With Asparagus

Prep time: 50mins   **Cook time: 0mins**

Servings: 2

Nutritional information:

Per serving: Kcal 165, Fat: 10g, Carbs: 10g, Protein: 8g

Ingredients		
→ 1/2 cup asparagus	→ Salt and pepper
→ 4 cups of arugula	→ 1/4 cup wine vinegar
→ 1/2 cup of raspberries	→ 1/4 cup raspberries
→ 2 ounces of almonds	→ 1/2 cup of olive oil
→ 1/4 cup of red onion	→ 1 shallot
→ 2 ounces of goat	

Direction

Arrange the asparagus, arugula, raspberries, almonds, goat cheese & red onion on 2 plates. To make the dressing, mix all of its ingredients in a food processor & blend well until smooth. Season with pepper & salt to taste. Extra dressing may be kept in the fridge for about a week. Lastly, drizzle dressing over your salads.

Salad Waldorf

Prep time: 5mins   **Cook time: 5mins**

Servings: 4

Nutritional information:

Per serving: Kcal 418, Fat: 35g, Carbs: 25g, Protein: 6g

Ingredients	
→ 2 tbsp. yogurt	→ 1 c. celery
→ 2 tbsp. of mayonnaise	→ Kosher salt
→ 1 tbsp. of lemon juice	→ 1/4 c. parsley
→ 1 c. apples	→ 1 cup walnuts
→ 1 c. red grapes	→ black pepper
→ Bibb lettuce	

Direction

Whisk together yogurt, mayonnaise, & lemon juice inside a large mixing bowl. Fold in the apple, grapes, celery, & parsley just until well incorporated. Sprinkle salt & pepper to taste. Serve onto lettuce with walnuts on the top.

Salad With Cucumber – Dill Cabbage & Lemon Seasoning

Prep time: 10mins   **Cook time: 0mins**

Servings: 8

Nutritional information:

Per serving: Kcal 96, Fat: 7g, Carbs: 7g, Protein: 1g

Ingredients		
→ 1 cucumber	→ 3 tbsp of Vinegar
→ 1 cabbage	→ One green onion
→ 4 tbsp dill	→ 4 tbsp of olive oil
→ 1/2 tsp of Salt	

Direction

Place the cabbage in a bowl & cut it into thin slices. Place the chopped dill, green onion & cucumber in a bowl with the cabbage. In a mixing bowl, put the salt, vinegar, & olive oil, toss well.

SALAD WITH FARFALLE CONFETTI

Prep time: 20mins   **Cook time: 0mins**

Servings: 5

Nutritional information:

Per serving: Kcal 354, Fat: 30g, Carbs: 17g, Protein: 3g

Ingredients	
→ 1 pint of grape tomatoes	→ ¼ cup red onion
→ 8 ounces shell pasta	→ 1 yellow chopped bell pepper
→ 2 cups spinach	→ Lemon Vinaigrette
→ 1 package feta cheese	→ 3 tablespoons dill

Direction

Drain pasta after cooking according to the instructions of the package. Toss the pasta, tomatoes &the rest of your ingredients. Serve right away, or refrigerate for about 8 hours.

SALAD WITH GINGER BEEF

Prep time: 25mins   **Cook time: 12mins**

Servings: 4

Nutritional information:

Per serving: Kcal 369, Fat: 22g, Carbs: 2g, Protein: 37g

Ingredients

→ 2 tablespoon ginger

→ 1½ lbs. of flank steak

→ ⅓ cup of brown sugar

→ 3 tablespoon of soy sauce

→ crushed garlic

→ ¼ cup of lime juice

→ baby greens

→ ¼ cup of olive oil

→ cucumber

→ Ginger Sesame

→ sesame seeds

→ scallions

→ cilantro

Direction

Marinate your steak for about an hour or until overnight in the marinade. Drain and filter the marinade. To make the salad, combine the cucumber, greens, scallions, cilantro & sesame seeds in a large mixing bowl. Broil or grill the steak until it reaches a medium doneness, approximately 6 minutes each side. Serve the meat sliced with some salad & dressing.

Salad With gr Pear

Prep time: 20mins   **Cook time: 0mins**

Servings: 6

Nutritional information:

Per serving: Kcal 240, Fat: 12g, Carbs: 29g, Protein: 6g

Ingredients

→ 3 tablespoons of apple cider vinegar

→ 1/2 cup of olive oil

→ 1/4 cup of sugar

→ 1/4 teaspoon of salt

→ 1/2 teaspoon of celery seed

→ Black pepper

→ 2 cups of frisée lettuce

→ 1/2 cup blue cheese

→ 2 heads of butter lettuce

→ 1/2 cup of walnuts

→ 2 pears

Direction

Collect the necessary items. In an air-tight jar with a cover, combine the vinegar, oil, sugar, salt, pepper & celery seed to make your dressing. Shake vigorously until your sugar has mixed fully & the dressing is well combined. Place it in the fridge until ready to be served. Toss the frisée, butter lettuce, pears, blue cheese & walnuts in a large dish lightly when prepared to dine. Toss the greens in the dressing to coat them. Serve right away and enjoy your dish.

Salad With Strawberry & Watercress With Almond Seasoning

Prep time: 20mins   **Cook time: 0mins**

Servings: 4

Nutritional information:

Per serving: Kcal 189, Fat: 10g, Carbs: 22g, Protein: 3g

Ingredients

→ 1 tablespoon lemon juice

→ 2 tablespoons of champagne vinegar

→ 1 teaspoon of honey

→ 1/4 cup of olive oil

→ Salt & pepper

→ 1/3 cup almonds

→ 1/2 cup mint or basil leaves

→ 1/2 cup crumbled feta

→ 1 bunch of watercress

→ 16 strawberries

→ 1 cucumber

→ 6 radishes

Direction

Preheat your oven to around 350 degrees Fahrenheit. Bake the almonds for about 7-9 minutes, until aromatic & golden, while using baking sheet. Allow to cool for a while. Whisk together the lemon juice, vinegar, honey, pepper & salt in a small mixing bowl. Whisk in some oil gradually. If desired, season with extra honey, pepper & salt. Toss half of the dressing with the mint & basil, watercress, strawberries, cucumber & radishes in a mixing bowl. Taste the salad and add more dressing if necessary until it is thoroughly covered and tasty. Serve with feta crumbles & toasted almonds on the top.

SEASONED PUMPKIN SEED CABBAGE SALAD

Prep time: 15mins   **Cook time: 0mins**

Servings: 4

Nutritional information:

Per serving: Kcal 90, Fat: 3g, Carbs: 15g, Protein: 3g

Ingredients	
→ 1/2 red cabbage	→ 3 tablespoons mayonnaise
→ 1 cabbage	→ 1/2 teaspoon black pepper
→ 1 carrot	
→ 2 tablespoons pumpkin seeds	→ 1 tablespoon of pickle juice
→ cranberries	→ 1 tablespoon of white vinegar
	→ 1/2 teaspoon of sea salt

Direction

Inside a large mixing bowl, combine the carrot, dried berries & cabbage put them aside. Take a small bowl whisk together the vinegar, mayonnaise, pickle juice, salt, pepper & sugar until well blended. Toss the salad in the dressing until it is thoroughly mixed. Refrigerate for about 30 mins to enable the flavors to mingle & develop fully. Before serving, toss in the roasted seeds of pumpkin and enjoy your salad.

Super Slaw

Nutritional information:

Per serving: Kcal 45, Fat: 1g, Carbs: 8g, Protein: 2g

Ingredients		
→ 1 apple	→ 2 tsp of Dijon mustard
→ ½ cabbage	→ ½ red onion
→ 2 carrots	→ 2 tsp of cider vinegar
→ 100g pot Greek yogurt	→ ½ lemon juice

Direction

Take a large salad mixing bowl combine the apple, cabbage, carrots, & onion in it. Combine the lemon juice, yogurt, vinegar, & mustard in another bowl. Season with pepper & salt, then drizzle over your veggies. Toss everything together to coat with the dressing well and serve right away, or refrigerate for a while, then serve.

TABBOULI

Prep time: 30mins   **Cook time: 0mins**

Servings: 8

Nutritional information:

Per serving: Kcal 165, Fat: 9g, Carbs: 20g, Protein: 3g

Ingredients

→ 6 spring onions	→ juice of 3 lemons
→ 150 g leaf parsley	→ 1 cup of bulgur
→ 4 tomatoes	→ 1/8 teaspoon black pepper
→ 5 tablespoons of olive oil	→ 1 cup of water
→ 1/8 teaspoon of salt	

Direction

Take a small mixing bowl, add a cup of boiling water & a cup full of bourghul, also known as bulgur. Cover the bowl with a towel to prevent the steam from escaping. Set aside for a while until completely cool. Place the spring onions, parsley, & tomatoes in another large mixing bowl and chop them finely. Pour the juice from all of your fresh lemons on the salad. Toss your salad well with black pepper, olive oil, and salt. Mix well with cooled bourghul & serve your food. Any leftovers should be stored in the refrigerator for up to two or three days.

THREE BEAN MANGO SALA

Prep time: 5mins   **Cook time: 5mins**

Servings: 6

Nutritional information:

Per serving: Kcal 336, Fat: 12g, Carbs: 45g, Protein: 14g

Ingredients	
→ 1 can of kidney beans	→ 1/2 bell pepper chopped
→ 1 can chickpeas	→ 1/4 cup red onions
→ 1 can of Northern beans	→ 1 clove garlic
→ 3/4 cup of dressing	→ 2 tablespoons cilantro

Direction

The three varieties of beans should be rinsed and well drained. Take a large mixing bowl combine all of the ingredients in it. Refrigerate while covered, for at least 2 hours, with stirring.

5.5 SMOOTHIES AND BEVERAGES

Amazing Blended Smoothie

Prep time: 5mins   **Cook time: 0mins**

Servings: 2

Nutritional information:

Per serving: Kcal 859, Fat: 15g, Carbs: 90g, Protein: 38g

Ingredients		
→ 1 c. strawberries	→ 1/2 cup of Greek yogurt	
→ 1 banana	→ 1 1/4 cup of almond milk	
→ 1 c. blackberries	→ 1 c. raspberries	

Direction

Take a blender, mix all of your ingredients in it and blend well. Transfer to 2 cups & top them with blackberries, then serve.

ANTIOXIDANT POWER JUICE

Prep time: 5mins   **Cook time: 2mins**

Servings: 2

Nutritional information:

Per serving: Kcal 58, Fat: 2g, Net Carbs: 5g, Protein: 2. 5g

Ingredients		
→ 1 cup of ice	→ 1 tsp of ginger powder
→ 1 stalk of celery around six inches long	→ 1 tsp of green powder
→ 1/2 cucumber Lebanese	→ 1 cup of water
→ 1 lime peeled	→ pinch of turmeric powder
→ 1 lettuce leaf	

Direction	
Add all the ingredients to a blender and pulse until it turns smooth for around 60 seconds.	

APPLE SMOOTHIE IN TEA

Prep time: 7mins   **Cook time: 0mins**

Servings: 1

Nutritional information:

Per serving: Kcal 400, Fat: 10g, Carbs: 78g, Protein: 6g

Ingredients		
→ 0.5 cup Coconut milk	→ 3 dates
→ 0.5 cup of Green Tea	→ 0.75 cup Kale
→ 0.5 apple	→ 1 tbsp of Peanut Butter
→ 0.5 Cinnamon	

Direction

Combine all of your ingredients and blend them in a blender until smooth. Then, serve.

APPLE SMOOTHIE WITH OATBERRIES

Prep time: 10mins   **Cook time: 0mins**

Servings: 1

Nutritional information:

Per serving: Kcal 388, Fat: 12g, Carbs: 97g, Protein: 5g

Ingredients	
→ 1/2 c berries (strawberries, blueberries, and blackberries)	→ 1/4 tsp of cinnamon
	→ ice
→ 1/2 c oatmeal	→ 1 Tbsp of wheat germ
→ ¼ c raspberry yogurt	→ 2 pkg of splenda
→ ¼ apple	→ 1 Tbsp flax
→ 1/3 cup of milk	

Direction

Take a blender, put all of your ingredients in it & pulse gradually. If required, add some ice in between & blend until you will reach your desired product, then serve.

BERRY BANANA SMOOTHIE

Prep time: 5mins   **Cook time: 0mins**

Servings: 2

Nutritional information:

Per serving: Kcal 203, Fat: 10.9g, Net Carbs: 22.9g, Protein: 6. 3g

Ingredients	
→ 1. 5 cups of almond milk → sweetener → 2 tbsp of flaxseeds	→ 1/2 frozen banana → 1. 5 cups of whole strawberries

Direction

Add liquid in a blender followed by flaxseeds and rest of ingredients with greens at last. Top with frozen fruit and blend for around 2minutes. Pour and serve in glasses.

Boston Emerald Smoothie

Prep time: 11mins   **Cook time: 0mins**

Servings: 3

Nutritional information:

Per serving: Kcal 90, Fat: 0.5g, Carbs: 19g, Protein: 3g

<table>
<tr><td rowspan="3">Ingredients</td><td>→ 3 pineapple</td><td>→ 2 cups spinach</td></tr>
<tr><td>→ 2 cups ice cubes</td><td>→ 1 stalk</td></tr>
<tr><td>→ ½ cup vanilla yogurt</td><td></td></tr>
</table>

Direction	Put all of your ingredients in a blender & cover it with the help of lid. Pulse it gradually, then add to the speed and blend for about 1 minute until your desired product is reached, then serve and enjoy your drink.

CHOCO CHERRIES SMOOTHIE

Prep time: 5mins   **Cook time: 0mins**

Servings: 1

Nutritional information:

Per Serving: Kcal 386, Fat: 13. 7g, Net Carbs: 53g, Protein: 15. 5g

Ingredients	→ 1/2 ripe avocado → 1 can full-fat coconut milk → 1 cup of frozen cherries	→ 1/4 cup of cacao powder → Filtered water and a few ice cubes → 1/4 tsp of turmeric

Direction	Add all the ingredients to a blender and blend until you get a smooth and creamy texture. Pour and serve in glasses.

Delicious Green Smoothie

Prep time: 5mins   **Cook time: 0mins**

Servings: 1

Nutritional information:

Per Serving: Kcal 380, Fat: 30g, Net Carbs: 13g, Protein: 12g

Ingredients

→ 2 cups of spinach

→ 2 brazil nuts

→ 10 almonds

→ 1 scoop of Greens Powder Amazing Grass

→ 1 cup of unsweetened coconut milk

→ 1 tbsp of potato starch

→ 1 scoop of Whey Protein Jarrow Formulas

Direction

Add first 4 ingredients in blender and blend until they turn smooth. Add rest of the ingredients and blend again.

Detoxifyng Green Tea

Prep time: 5mins   **Cook time: 7mins**

Servings: 2

Nutritional information:

Per serving: Kcal 1, Fat: 0.2g, Carbs: 0g, Protein: 1g

Ingredients		
→ 2 green tea bags	→ ¼ teaspoon honey
→ 2 cups of water	→ 1 teaspoon ginger
→ 1 lemon	→ ⅛ teaspoon of turmeric
→ ⅛ - ¼ teaspoon cayenne pepper	→ ⅛ teaspoon of cinnamon

Direction

Combine the green tea-bags, water, lemon juice, ginger, cinnamon, cayenne pepper, turmeric, & agave nectar or honey in a saucepan or teapot over medium flame. Bring it to boil, then reduce to a low flame to let flavors merge completely, approximately for 5 minutes. Then, pour the mixture into cups. Drink immediately if you want, or keep in the refrigerator for later use.

GREEN GOBLIN

Prep time: 2mins   **Cook time: 0mins**

Servings: 1

Nutritional information:

Per serving: Kcal 300, Fat: 0g, Carbs: 0g, Protein: 0g

Ingredients	
→ 1 ounce of coconut rum	→ 1 ounce of peach schnapps
→ 1 ounce of vodka	→ 1 ounce sweet-and-sour mix
→ ginger ale	→ 1 ounce of sour apple liqueur

Direction

Put all of your ingredients in a blender; also add ice cubes in it. Blend well, then pour in your glass with some extra ice cubes as well. Serve it with the wedges of lime.

JUICE FROM CRUCIFEROUS PLANTS

Prep time: 7mins   **Cook time: 0mins**

Servings: 2

Nutritional information:

Per serving: Kcal 219, Fat: 2g, Carbs: 4g, Protein: 6g

Ingredients

→ 2 bananas

→ 1.5 cups milk or water

→ 2 cups kale

→ 3/4 cup of strawberries

→ 1 cup of cauliflower

→ 1/2 cup of mango

→ 2 tbsp flax seeds

→ 2 tbsp of hemp hearts

→ 1/3 cup of pomegranate arils

→ 1/8 tsp of black pepper

→ 1/2 tsp of turmeric

Direction

Pour all of your ingredients in a blender, then blend until creamy & smooth.

ORANGE SHERBET BLENDED SMOOTHIE

Prep time: 5mins   **Cook time: 0mins**

Servings: 4

Nutritional information:

Per serving: Kcal 127, Fat: 1.1g, Carbs: 29g, Protein: 1.6g

Ingredients	→ 1 cup of orange sherbet → ½ cup of orange juice → ½ teaspoon of vanilla	→ 1 ½ cups of peaches → 1 cup of banana

Direction	Place all of your ingredients in a blender and blend them well, then serve.

SMOOTHIE OF WATERMELON & RASPBERRIE

Prep time: 10mins   **Cook time: 0mins**

Servings: 4

Nutritional information:

Per serving: Kcal 102, Fat: 1g, Carbs: 18g, Protein: 7g

Ingredients		
→ ½ cup of water	→ ½ cup raspberries
→ 1 ¾ cups of skim milk	→ 4 sprigs mint
→ 3 cups watermelon cubes	→ 1 teaspoon lime juice
→ ½ cup yogurt	→ 4 slices watermelon

Direction

Put all of your smoothie ingredients in blender; also add water if required and blend them well until your desired consistency. Transfer to glasses, then garnish them with watermelon wedges & mint sprigs. Serve right away.

Smoothie Coconut and Greens

Prep time: 5mins   **Cook time: 0mins**

Servings: 1

Nutritional information:

Per serving: Kcal 251, Fat: 11g, Carbs: 24g, Protein: 12g

Ingredients	
→ 1/2 cup Greek yogurt	→ 1 green apple
→ 1/2 cup of coconut milk	→ 1 banana peeled
→ 1 cup of spinach	→ 2 tablespoons coconut
→ 1 cup of ice	

Direction

Put all of your ingredients in blender, also add ice at last and blend them well, then serve right away.

Smoothie With Blueberry & Pineapple

Prep time: 5mins   **Cook time: 0mins**

Servings: 2

Nutritional information:

Per serving: Kcal 153, Fat: 2g, Carbs: 35g, Protein: 2g

<table>
<tr><td rowspan="2" style="writing-mode: vertical-lr">Ingredients</td><td>→ 1 cup almond milk</td><td>→ 1 cup blueberries</td></tr>
<tr><td>→ 1 cup pineapple chunks</td><td>→ 1 banana</td></tr>
</table>

Direction

Put all of your ingredients in blender & blend until you will reach your desired product. Add fresh blueberries & banana slices to garnish, then serve.

SMOOTHIE WITH SPICED MANGO

Prep time: 2mins   **Cook time: 15mins**

Servings: 2

Nutritional information:

Per serving: Kcal 190, Fat: 12g, Carbs: 84g, Protein: 7g

Ingredients	
→ 1 tbsp Greek yoghurt	→ 2 cm of root ginger
→ 1 mango,	→ ½orange
→ 300 ml of almond milk	→ ¼ tsp cinnamon
→ ground turmeric	

Direction	
Take a blender, and blend all of your smoothie ingredients in it. Transfer it to two glasses, then serve with some cinnamon on the top.	

TURMERIC ORANGE JUICE

Prep time: 10mins **Cook time: 0mins**

Servings: 2

Nutritional information:

Per serving: Kcal 250, Fat: 1g, Carbs: 61g, Protein: 5g

Ingredients	→ 2 inches of Turmeric → 4 Carrots	→ 4 Oranges

Direction	Wash & then chop all of your ingredients, then put in the juicer. So, juice them well & enjoy your drink.

TURMERIC REFRESHER

Prep time: 7mins   **Cook time: 0mins**

Servings: 2

Nutritional information:

Per serving: Kcal 241, Fat: 0.7g, Carbs: 60g, Protein: 2g

Ingredients		
	→ 1 pinch turmeric	→ ½ cup Orange Juice
	→ ½ inch grated ginger	→ 2 tbsp. of honey

Direction	
	Mix all of your ingredients until well combined. Then transfer to a normal glass & drink right away.

5.6 Soups & Stews

ACORN SQUASH STEW WITH BRUSSELS SPROUTS

Prep time: 20mins   **Cook time: 40mins**

Servings: 6

Nutritional information:

Per serving: Kcal 333, Fat: 10g, Carbs: 52g, Protein: 11g

Ingredients

→ 1 tablespoon olive oil

→ 1 cup spelt

→ 1 cup onion

→ ⅓ cup celery

→ ½ cup carrot

→ 3 ounces pancetta

→ 5 cups chicken broth

→ Two garlic cloves,

→ ⅓ cup white wine

→ 1 ounce of Romano cheese

→ 1 cup butternut squash

→ 1 ½ cups chestnuts

→ 1 cup Brussels sprouts

→ 1 cup grape tomatoes, halved

→ ¼ teaspoon black pepper

Direction

Inside a large frying pan, combine the spelt and the water. Bring them to boil with 2 inches of water over the spelt. Reduce heat to low and cook for about 20 minutes, or until vegetables are soft. Drain the water and put it aside. In an oven, heat the oil over medium heat. Sauté for about 8 mins, or until carrot, onion, celery, garlic & pancetta are aromatic and starting to brown. Scrape pan to release browned pieces before adding wine & broth. Bring to the boil with the squash, chestnuts, Brussels sprouts, & pepper. Reduce your flame, and let it simmer, for about 10 minutes, uncovered. Then cover it & simmer for about 10 minutes more after adding the tomatoes & spelt. Pour 1 cup of soup to each of your bowls and top them with cheese equally.

ASPARAGUS CREAM SOUP

Prep time: 15mins   **Cook time: 25mins**

Servings: 4

Nutritional information:

Per serving: Kcal 196, Fat: 13g, Carbs: 14g, Protein: 6g

Ingredients	
→ ½ cup onion	→ 2 tablespoons of butter
→ 1 pound of asparagus	→ 1 teaspoon of salt
→ 1 can of chicken broth	→ 1 cup of milk
→ 1 teaspoon lemon juice	→ 1 pinch black pepper
→ 2 tablespoons flour	→ ½ cup of sour cream

Direction

Combine sliced onion, asparagus & chicken stock in a frying pan. Bring it to boil, covered, over high flame. Reduce your flame to low and cook, uncovered, for about 12 minutes, until the asparagus is soft. To purée all veggies, blend your mixture inside a blender. Let it sit aside. Melt some butter in a frying pan over low flame. Combine the salt, flour and pepper in it. Cook for about 2 minutes, stirring regularly. Increase your flame to medium & mix in the leftover chicken stock. Cook until this mixture boils, stirring regularly. Add the milk & asparagus puree in it. Take a bowl, add sour cream in it and mix in your heated soup. Stir the soup with the lemon juice & mix of sour cream. Allow it to cook slowly while stirring constantly, but do not let it boil. Serve right away.

BLACK FOREST SOUP WITH MUSHROOMS IN CREAM

Prep time: 20mins   **Cook time: 25mins**

Servings: 6

Nutritional information:

Per serving: Kcal 225, Fat: 2g, Carbs: 41g, Protein: 9g

Ingredients

- 3 tsp of Garlic
- 1 cup Mushrooms
- 5.7 cup of Bolthouse Farms Juice
- 2 carrot
- 3 cups of Almond Milk
- 1 cup Onion
- 2 stalks of Celery
- 1.34 cup Vegetables, Super Sweet Corn
- 12.5 tsp of Seasoning Salute
- 6 tsp of thyme
- 2 tsp Herb Seasoning
- 0.25 cup of Lemon Juice
- 6 tsp of Rosemary
- 1 cup of Spinach
- 2 cup Cannellini Beans

Direction

Bring milk, carrot juice, carrots, celery, seasoning & onion to boil inside a large cooking-pot. Reduce your flame to low and cook for about 30 minutes. For approximately 5 mins, sauté the garlic, mushrooms & Italian seasoning. Keep aside for a while. After the soup has finished simmering, puree it using a blender. Return the purée to your pot. Toss in the spinach, remaining herbs, sautéed mushrooms & beans. Heat until the spinach is completely wilted.

BROCCOLI MUSHROOMS BISQUE

Prep time: 20mins   **Cook time: 45mins**

Servings: 8

Nutritional information:

Per serving: Kcal 69, Fat: 2g, Carbs: 11g, Protein: 4g

Ingredients	
→ 1 tablespoon of canola oil	→ 2 celery ribs
→ 1 bunch of broccolis	→ 1 garlic clove
→ 1/2 pound of mushrooms	→ 1/4 cup onion
→ 2 carrots	→ 2 cups of water
→ 1 tablespoon soy sauce	→ 1 carton vegetable broth
→ 2 tablespoons of lemon juice	

Direction

Broccoli florets should be cut into small pieces. Stalks should be peeled and well chopped. Heat oil in a big frying pan over medium flame and cook mushrooms until soft, for about 4 to 6 minutes. Remove your pan from the heat, then stir some soy sauce in it. Bring carrots, broccoli stalks, celery, garlic, onion, broth, & water to boil in a frying pan. Reduce your flame to low and cook, uncovered, for around 25 to 30 mins, or until your veggies become softened. Using a blender, puree your soup. Alternatively, allow to cool a little, then purée the soup inside a blender before returning it to the pan. Bring it to boil with the mushrooms & florets. Reduce flame to medium and simmer, while stirring, for about 8-10 mins, or until your broccoli is cooked. Add the lemon juice, mix well and serve.

CREAMY ZUCCHINI SOUP

Prep time: 5mins   **Cook time: 20mins**

Servings: 4

Nutritional information:

Per serving: Kcal 60, Fat: 1g, Carbs: 10g, Protein: 3.5g

Ingredients

→ 2 cloves of garlic

→ 1/2 onion

→ parmesan cheese

→ 3 zucchinis

→ 2 tbsp sour cream

→ 32 oz chicken broth,

→ kosher salt & black pepper

Direction

Take a large cooking pot, place it over medium flame, bring the chicken stock, garlic, and zucchini & onion to the boil. Reduce the heat to low, cover, & cook for approximately 20 mins, or until the vegetables are soft. Remove it from the flame and puree with the help of a blender, then put some sour cream & puree once again until your desired consistency. Season pepper & salt according to your taste then, serve right away.

Crunchy Sweet Potato Stew

Prep time: 25mins   **Cook time: 30mins**

Servings: 6

Nutritional information:

Per serving: Kcal 252, Fat: 5g, Carbs: 45g, Protein: 6.9g

Ingredients	
→ 3 cups of vegetable broth	→ 1 tablespoon of lemon juice
→ 3 cups sweet potatoes	→ 1 teaspoon of ground cumin
→ 2 teaspoons of olive oil	→ 1 teaspoon coriander
→ 1 stalk of celery	→ 2 tablespoons of peanut butter
→ 1 cup onion	→ 1 teaspoon of curry powder
→ ½ cup red bell pepper	→ 1 teaspoon of chili powder
→ 1 can chickpeas	→ ¼ teaspoon of pepper
→ 1 clove of garlic	→ ½ teaspoon of salt
→ 1 can tomatoes	→ ½ cup of raisins
→ 2 teaspoons grated ginger	

Direction

Add a small amount of broth to your sweet potatoes while taking a dish safe for microwave. And microwave for about 3-5 minutes, or until softened lightly. In a cooking pot, heat the olive oil on medium flame. Combine the celery, onion, bell pepper, & garlic in it. Cook for about 3-5 minutes, stirring occasionally. Add your sweet potatoes, already softened, the rest of the broth, the chickpeas, the tomatoes, the lemon juice, the ginger, curry powder, cumin, coriander, salt, chilli powder, & some pepper. Bring it to boil, then lower your flame to a low heat & cover it. Then, cook for approximately 20 mins, or until your veggies are soft. Add some peanut butter & raisins in your soup & simmer for about 5 more minutes. Add spices if needed, then serve hot.

DETOXIFYNG BEET & GAZPACHO SOUP

Prep time: 45mins   **Cook time: 30mins**

Servings: 2

Nutritional information:

Per serving: Kcal 367, Fat: 20g, Carbs: 42g, Protein: 5.4g

Ingredients	
→ 1 red pepper	→ 1 head of cilantro
→ handful beet	→ 3–4 cups of water
→ 1 carrot	→ 1–2 cloves of garlic
→ 1 cucumber	→ 2 tablespoons protein powder
→ 2 stalks celery	
→ 1 avocado	→ cayenne pepper
→ 1 lemon Juice	→ Celtic sea salt

Direction

Put all of your ingredients in a blender and blend well till smooth & super creamy. Serve immediately, or you can also chill for few hrs if desired. Top your soup with hemp seeds & sprouts and enjoy it.

FUHRMAN'S FAMOUS SOUP

Prep time: 60mins   **Cook time: 30mins**

Servings: 10

Nutritional information:

Per serving: Kcal 224, Fat: 7.4g, Carbs: 32g, Protein: 11g

Ingredients

- → 4 cups of water
- → 1 cup peas
- → 4 onions
- → 3 leeks
- → 6 -10 zucchini
- → 2 bunches of collard greens
- → 2 bunches of organic celery
- → 8 ounces of mushrooms
- → 5 lbs. of organic carrots
- → 1 cup cashews
- → 2 tablespoons seasoning

Direction

On a low heat, add the water & beans to a big cooking pot.

Toss in onions, zucchini, leeks, as well as chopped kale to the pot. Also, add celery juice, carrot juice, and your seasoning. Cook for about 20 minutes or until your veggies are tender. Transfer this mixture to your blender and blend the veggies completely. Toss in a little more liquid from the soup, also with the cashews, and blend for a few more minutes. Transfer it to your soup pot. Then, cook for a further 30 minutes by adding mushrooms in it and serve.

HOMEMADE VEGGIE SOUP

Prep time: 10mins   **Cook time: 30mins**

Servings: 5

Nutritional information:

Per serving: Kcal 137, Fat: 5.7g, Carbs: 20g, Protein: 3.2g

Ingredients

→ 2 cups onion

→ 3 tablespoons of olive oil

→ 1 ½ cups carrot

→ 2 tablespoons of tomato paste

→ 1 ½ cups celery

→ 4 teaspoons garlic

→ 1/2 teaspoon black pepper

→ 3/4 teaspoon fennel seed

→ 1/2 teaspoon sea salt

→ 1 can tomatoes

→ 1/8 teaspoon red pepper flakes

→ 6 cups of stock or broth

→ 1/2 teaspoon of apple cider vinegar

→ 3 to 4 cups cabbage

→ 2 cups potato

→ 1 cup peas

→ Two bay leaves

Direction

Inside a cooking pot, heat the oil over medium flame. Combine the carrots, onions, celery, & tomato paste in it. Cook, while stirring often, for about 8-10 mins, or until your veggies have completely softened. Combine the fennel, garlic, black pepper, flakes of red pepper and some salt in it. Cook for a minute, stirring constantly. Mix in the stock, as well as your tinned tomatoes along with the juice. Also, put the cabbage potatoes with bay leaves. Bring it to boil by increasing the flame to high. Cook, stirring occasionally, for about 20 minutes, until your vegetables are soft. Cook for another five minutes after adding frozen peas. Discard bay leaves & turn off the heat. Add the apple cider vinegar and mix well. Season with extra pepper, salt, or vinegar according to your taste and enjoy.

Medley of Corn and Beans

Nutritional information:

> Per serving: Kcal 137, Fat: 4g, Carbs: 19g, Protein: 7g

Ingredients

- → 1/3 cup onion
- → 1 green pepper
- → 1-1/2 teaspoons of butter
- → 1-3/4 cups corn
- → 1/8 teaspoon of cayenne pepper
- → 1-1/2 teaspoons of olive oil
- → 1-1/2 cups edamame
- → 1/4 teaspoon of garlic salt
- → 3/4 cup black beans

Direction

Onion & green pepper should be sauteed in oil or butter and oil in a frying pan until soft. Combine all of your leftover ingredients and stir well. Cook, stirring constantly, for about 4-5 minutes, then serve.

Qu Kale Soup

Nutritional information:

Per serving: Kcal 262, Fat: 6.2g, Carbs: 26g, Protein: 26g

Ingredients	
→ 1 onion	→ 1 can tomatoes
→ 2 tbsp. olive oil	→ 1 cup of quinoa
→ 2 carrots	→ red pepper flakes
→ 3 cloves of garlic	→ 8 c. vegetable broth
→ 2 stalks of celery	→ 1/2 tsp. of ground cumin
→ 1 zucchini	→ 1 tbsp. lemon juice
→ 1 can of cannellini beans	→ 8 oz. Tuscan kale

Direction

Heat the oil in a cooking pot on medium flame. Season with pepper & salt; also put carrot, onion, celery, & some garlic. Cook, while stirring periodically, for approximately 10 mins or until your veggies are tender. Mix chopped tomatoes, zucchini, beans, cumin & quinoa in it. Pour your broth & mix well. Bring it to boil, then reduce and cook until the quinoa is cooked, for approximately 13 minutes. Cook for a minute longer after adding the kale, then add the lemon juice. Serve with a pinch of pepper, salt & flakes of red pepper.

Quick Homemade Tomato Gazpacho

Prep time: 25mins　　　**Cook time: 0mins**

Servings: 6

Nutritional information:

Per serving: Kcal 181, Fat: 14g, Carbs: 13g, Protein: 3g

Ingredients	
→ 1 cucumber	→ ¼ cup fresh basil
→ 2 ½ pounds tomatoes	→ 2 tablespoons red-wine vinegar
→ 1 red bell pepper	
→ 3 tablespoons olive oil	→ 1/2 teaspoon ground pepper
→ 1 clove garlic	→ 1 teaspoon salt
	→ 1 avocado

Direction

Slice one over forth of your total cucumber, tomatoes and bell pepper and set them aside. Take a blender purée the leftover cucumber, tomatoes, & bell pepper with garlic, vinegar, oil, salt, & some pepper until creamy. Pour into a big mixing bowl, and let it chill for approx. 2 hours. Before serving, cut the avocado & mix it with the chopped veggies that have been set aside. Add the basil, the leftover oil, some vinegar, &a bit of pepper and salt. Pour the gazpacho in soup bowls with your chopped veggie salad and enjoy.

5.7 Appetizers & Snacks

BAKED EGGPLANTS

Prep time: 15mins   **Cook time: 30mins**

Servings: 6

Nutritional information:

Per serving: Kcal 54, Fat: 3g, Carbs: 3.2g, Protein: 2.4g

Ingredients

→ 1 eggplant

→ cooking spray

→ 3 tomatoes,

→ salt and black pepper

→ 1 teaspoon of oregano

→ 1 tablespoon olive oil

→ ⅓ cup Parmesan cheese

Direction

Preheat your oven to around 400 degrees Fahrenheit. Use foil to line your baking dish. In the base of your baking dish, arrange the slices of tomato & eggplant. Sprinkle using salt, pepper, and some oregano; also, pour olive oil on the veggies. Parmesan cheese should be sprinkled over the whole mixture. Bake for about 30 minutes in a pre-heated oven till the cheese begins to brown. Adjust the broiler of your oven to high and bake for another 5 minutes, or until thoroughly browned.

Baked Garlic Dip

Prep time: 10mins   **Cook time: 60mins**

Servings: 8

Nutritional information:

Per serving: Kcal 243, Fat: 24g, Carbs: 5g, Protein: 2g

Ingredients

→ 3 tbsp of Olive Oil	→ ½ cup of Mayonnaise
→ 3 heads of Garlic	→ ½ teaspoon of Dried Thyme
→ 1 ½ cup of Sour Cream	→ ½ teaspoon of Salt
→ ½ teaspoon of Dried Rosemary	→ 3 tablespoons of Chopped Parsley
→ 3 tablespoons of Lemon Juice	→ ½ teaspoon Black Pepper

Direction

Preheat your oven to around 400 degrees Fahrenheit. Cut off the top of each garlic head to reveal the cloves. Drizzle some olive oil over each garlic head. Wrap with aluminum foil around each garlic head separately. Roast the cloves in an oven for about 1 hour or until they are tender. Allow 20 to 30 minutes for cooling. Squeeze all of the cloves out now and place in a container after they have cooled. Using the fork, mash them. Mix in the sour cream well. Dried rosemary, mayonnaise, dried thyme, salt, parsley, black pepper, & lemon juice are added to the mixture. Combine the ingredients well. Refrigerate for about one hour prior to serving.

BREAD MADE WITH CORN

Servings: 12

Nutritional information:

Per serving: Kcal 189, Fat: 7.4g, Carbs: 28g, Protein: 3g

Ingredients	
→ 1 cup cornmeal	→ 3 ½ teaspoons of baking powder
→ 1 cup flour	→ 1 teaspoon of salt
→ ⅔ cup sugar	→ 1 cup of milk
→ ⅓ cup of vegetable oil	→ 1 egg

Direction

Preheat your oven to around 400 degrees Fahrenheit. Spray a round shaped cake pan with the help of cooking spray. Take a large bowl add cornmeal, flour, sugar, baking powder & salt in it. Also, add milk, egg, & vegetable oil and stir well until combined. Drizzle batter in lined pan. Bake for about 20-25 minutes in a pre-heated oven and then serve.

CHICKEN CROSTINI WITH ROASTED RED PEPPER

Prep time: 17mins   **Cook time: 17mins**

Servings: 6

Nutritional information:

Per serving: Kcal 168, Fat: 15g, Carbs: 3.3g, Protein: 5g

Ingredients	
→ 1/3 cup smoked mozzarella → 2 tablespoons of olive oil	→ 6 slices of baguette → 1/2 cup strips of red bell pepper

Direction

Preheat your oven to around 375 degrees Fahrenheit. Place the pieces of bread on your baking sheet & arrange them. Brush the bread pieces with some oil. Bake for around 15 minutes, or until light golden & crisp. On top of the toast, place the strips of bell pepper. Cheese should be sprinkled on top. Broil for 2 more minutes until your cheese melts.

Cookies With Meringue

Prep time: 15mins   **Cook time: 40mins**

Servings: 24

Nutritional information:

Per serving: Kcal 10, Fat: 0g, Carbs: 2g, Protein: 0g

Ingredients	
→ 3/4 cup sugar	→ 3 egg whites
→ 1/2 teaspoon of vanilla extract	→ 1/8 teaspoon of cream of tartar

Direction

Preheat your oven to around 200 degrees Fahrenheit and line two baking dishes with foil. Combine the vanilla, egg whites, and tartar cream with sugar spoon by spoon together and whisk well. Whisk for extra 5 mins after putting all of your sugar's desired quantity. Pour the batter in a large bag of pastry fitted with a big tip of star. Pipe 2 inches of your cookies onto baking pans coated with parchment paper, allowing an inch among each cookie. Then, bake the cookies for about 45 minutes, and take off the pan from a heat and let it cool fully before keeping in a sealed container.

Corn With grilled & Spicy Kettle

Prep time: 5mins   **Cook time: 15mins**

Servings: 5

Nutritional information:

Per serving: Kcal 209, Fat: 11g, Carbs: 24g, Protein: 2.4g

Ingredients	→ ½ cup popcorn kernels → ¼ cup of white sugar	→ ¼ cup of vegetable oil

Direction	Put a large saucepan over medium flame, heat vegetable oil in it. Toss in the popcorn and sugar after the pan is heated. To protect your sugar from igniting, cover the pan and shake gently. Remove the pan from flame after the popping sound has slowed and slightly shake for another few mins till popping has completely ceased. Allow to cool in a large sized bowl, stirring regularly to break any big clumps.

DIP WITH CHEESE & HERBS

Prep time: 7mins   **Cook time: 0mins**

Servings: 6

Nutritional information:

Per serving: Kcal 279, Fat: 21g, Carbs: 3g, Protein: 15g

Ingredients	
→ ¼ cup of mixed herbs	→ ground pepper
→ 12 oz cheese	→ olive oil
→ cracker	→ Crudité
→ ¾ cup of white wine	

Direction

Take a food-processor, combine the herbs & cheese in it & pulse till chopped finely. Add some wine and again pulse for about 30 to 45 seconds, or until creamy. Take a dish, scoop the mixture of your cheese, pour some olive oil, then season with some pepper. Serve with crackers & crudités at room temperature and enjoy the food.

ICE MILK WITH CANDIED GINGER

Prep time: 10mins   **Cook time: 5mins**

Servings: 3

Nutritional information:

Per serving: Kcal 276, Fat: 21g, Carbs: 23g, Protein: 2.2g

Ingredients

→ ½ cup of cream of coconut

→ 3 cups of coconut milk

→ One 1-inch piece of ginger

→ 2 teaspoons turmeric

→ ¼ cup of honey

→ ½ teaspoon cinnamon

→ ¼ teaspoon cardamom

→ Candied ginger

→ ½ teaspoon salt

→ 1 vanilla bean

→ ¼ teaspoon black pepper

Direction

Bring your ingredients, except candied ginger, to a simmering in a frying pan over medium flame. Allow to cool fully before storing in the refrigerator overnight. Make absolutely sure the ice cream-maker's-bowl is frozen throughout this time. Put the base to the ice cream-maker's-bowl the following day and churn it according to instructions of manufacturer. Freeze for about 4 hours after scraping onto a dish. Pour the honey over your ice-cream in bowls. Serve with candied ginger.

ICE POPS WITH BLUEBERRIES & CREAM

Prep time: 15mins   **Cook time: 0mins**

Servings: 8

Nutritional information:

Per serving: Kcal 112, Fat: 3g, Carbs: 22g, Protein: 0g

Ingredients	
→ 2/3 cup of water	→ 1/4 cup whipping cream
→ 8 freezer pop molds	→ 2 cups blueberries
→ 2/3 cup of sugar	

Direction

To make sugar syrup, put water & some sugar in a frying pan and bring it to boil, stirring constantly. Allow to cool fully. Meanwhile, finely puree blueberries in a mixing bowl also whisk in sugar syrup & cream. Fill paper cups or molds with the mixture. Use holders for covering the molds. If you're using cups, cover them with foil & poke the sticks into the foil. Freeze until the mixture is solid. Unmold them and serve.

Kale Chips

Prep time: 10mins   **Cook time: 10mins**

Servings: 6

Nutritional information:

Per serving: Kcal 58, Fat: 2.8g, Carbs: 7g, Protein: 2.5g

Ingredients	→ 1 teaspoon of seasoned salt → 1 tablespoon of olive oil	→ 1 bunch kale

Direction

Preheat your oven to around 350 degrees Fahrenheit. Using parchment paper, line a non-stick baking sheet. Remove the leaves off the thick stems with a knife & split into bite-size pieces. Using a salad spinner, thoroughly dry the washed kale. Pour olive oil over the greens and season with salt. Bake for around 10-15 minutes, or until slightly golden.

TORTILLA CHIPS WITH CINNAMON

Prep time: 10mins   **Cook time: 10mins**

Servings: 8

Nutritional information:

Per serving: Kcal 96, Fat: 6g, Carbs: 10g, Protein: 1g

Ingredients	→ ¼ cup of unsalted butter → 1 tsp of cinnamon	→ 1 package of flour tortillas → ¼ cup of granulated sugar

Direction	Preheat your oven to around 350°F. Melt the butter and brush it on the tortillas. In a mixing bowl, combine the sugar & cinnamon. Season over the tortillas. Cut your tortillas into slices and arrange the triangles on a baking. To help this procedure go quickly and easily, try to use pizza cutter. Then, bake for about 8-10 minutes, or until golden brown and crispy. Serve them with a fruit salsa.

5.8 Desserts

CHIA PUDDING WITH MANGO, TURMERIC AND COCONUT

Prep time: 10mins   **Cook time: 0mins**

Servings: 2

Nutritional information:

Per serving: Kcal 224, Fat: 6g, Carbs: 40g, Protein: 8g

Ingredients	
→ 1 cup of coconut milk	→ 1/ 2 teaspoon of turmeric
→ 1 mango	→ 1 tablespoon of maple syrup
→ Kiwi	→ Coconut chips
→ 5 tablespoons of chia seeds	→ Coconut yogurt

Direction

Inside a blender, puree the mango till smooth. If you're going to use frozen mango, thaw it first. In a mixing bowl, combine the puree of mango & the other ingredients and whisk until no lumps left. Allow to sit for about 5 minutes before stirring again. Refrigerate over-night, while covered. Serve in two glasses with a dollop of coconut or natural yogurt, kiwi & mango chunks, and a sprinkling of coconut.

Couscous Pudding With Vanilla

Prep time: 15mins   **Cook time: 10mins**

Servings: 4

Nutritional information:

Per serving: Kcal 235, Fat: 2g, Carbs: 44g, Protein: 11g

Ingredients

→ ½ cup couscous

→ 4 teaspoons of maple syrup

→ ⅔ cup of water

→ ¼ teaspoon of salt

→ ¼ cup brown sugar

→ 3 cups milk

→ ½ teaspoon of vanilla extract

→ 1 egg

Direction

Bring water to the boil, then add the couscous and some salt in it. Remove the pot from the heat, cover, and set aside for about 5 minutes. Bring the sugar & milk to a boil. Reduce flame to low and whisk until the liquid has thickened somewhat. Put in a mixing bowl and whisk your egg in it. Return to your pan, stirring constantly, until the mixture is creamy. Transfer it to another bowl and add some vanilla in it. Allow pudding to cool for a while, stirring every now and again. Pour into your bowls & chill for about an hour, lightly covered. Before serving, drizzle it with some maple syrup.

Custard With Sweet Cinnamon

Prep time: 20mins   **Cook time: 20mins**

Servings: 4

Nutritional information:

Per serving: Kcal 130, Fat: 3g, Carbs: 23g, Protein: 4g

<table>
<tr><td rowspan="2">Ingredients</td><td>→ 2 eggs</td><td>→ Whipped cream</td></tr>
<tr><td>→ 1 ½ cups of diced carrots

→ ⅓ - ½ cup brown sugar</td><td>→ ½ teaspoon cinnamon

→ ¼ cup milk</td></tr>
</table>

Direction

Preheat your oven to around 350 degrees Fahrenheit. Place 4 cups of custard in baking pan and lightly oil them. Leave aside. Meanwhile, in a frying pan, add chopped carrots & some water. Bring it to boil, then turn off the heat. Cook with a lid on for about 20-25 mins or until the veggies are soft. Drain, then rinse with some cold water. In a food-processor, puree the carrots. Lid on and continue for approx. 20 seconds, or till the mixture is completely smooth. Cover & again process the brown sugar, eggs, milk, & cinnamon until creamy. Divide the carrot mixture equally among the ramekins that have been prepared. Place the baking pan on the middle rack of the oven. Fill the baking-pan partly with boiling water to achieve halfway up the edges of the ramekins. Then, bake for about 30 to 35 minutes. Allow to cool for a while. Serve with some whipped cream if preferred. Within wot hours, chill, then serve.

GRANITA D'APPLE TART

Prep time: 20mins   **Cook time: 45mins**

Servings: 8

Nutritional information:

Per serving: Kcal 467, Fat: 25g, Carbs: 58g, Protein: 5g

Ingredients

- → 1/3 cup brown sugar
- → 1/3 cup of sugar
- → 1/4 cup flour
- → 1/4 teaspoon ginger
- → 1 teaspoon cinnamon
- → 1/4 teaspoon nutmeg
- → 1 tablespoon of lemon juice

- → 6 to 7 cups tart apples
- → Coarse sugar or Turbinado, ground cinnamon, caramel sauce and vanilla bean ice cream
- → Double-crust pie Dough
- → 1 egg white
- → 1 tablespoon of butter

Direction

Preheat the oven to around 375 degrees Fahrenheit. Roll the dough one half into a broad circle on the slightly floured surface and put to your pie dish. Combine the flour, sugars, & spices inside mixing bowl. Toss lime juice with apples in another mixing bowl. Toss in the mix of sugar to coat well. Fill with filling & butter. Roll out the rest of your dough into a broad circle. Place on top of the filling. Edges should be trimmed, sealed, and fluted. Make slits in the top. Brush the crust with an egg white that has been beaten till fluffy. Season with ground cinnamon & turbinado sugar, if preferred. Cover the edge using the foil. 25 minutes in the oven & discard the foil again bake for another 20 to 25 mins. Allow to cool on the wire rack. Serve atop ice cream with caramel sauce, if preferred.

GREEK YOGURT WITH WALNUTS FRUIT

Prep time: 5mins   **Cook time: 0mins**

Servings: 1

Nutritional information:

Per serving: Kcal 93, Fat: 2.7g, Carbs: 9g, Protein: 8g

Ingredients	
→ 1 ½ teaspoons walnuts → ⅓ cup Greek yogurt	→ 3 apricots

Direction

Put yogurt by taking a bowl, then mix in some apricots, also put walnuts & serve.

Pavlova With Peaches

Prep time: 25mins   **Cook time: 80mins**

Servings: 16

Nutritional information:

Per serving: Kcal 253, Fat: 14g, Carbs: 29g, Protein: 2.7g

Ingredients	
→ 1 2/3 cups of caster sugar	→ 1 tsp of white vinegar
→ Six egg whites	→ 300g raspberries
→ 1 tsp of vanilla extract	→ 600ml cream
→ 825g can of peach slices	→ 1 tbsp of icing sugar mixture
→ 2 tsp of corn flour	

Direction

Preheat the oven to around 120 degrees Celsius. Using baking paper, line a baking pan. On a piece of paper, draw a rectangle. Egg whites should be whisked until soft using the electric-mixer. 1 tbsp turn by turn, whisk in caster-sugar until completely dissolved. Combine the vanilla, cornflour & vinegar in a mixing bowl. 1 minute of beating, then pour the mixture into the tray that has been prepared. Spread the mixture in the indicated rectangle using a spatula. Bake for about 1 hour & 20 minutes, until firm. Turn your off oven. Allow it cool in the oven with the door slightly open. Inside a food-processor, combine the raspberries & sugar. Blend until completely smooth. Arrange pavlova on a serving plate. Finish with a dollop of sour cream, peaches, and the last of the raspberries. Drizzle the raspberry mixture over the top. Serve.

Peaches Baked With Cream Cheese

Prep time: 1mins   **Cook time: 9mins**

Servings: 4

Nutritional information:

Per serving: Kcal 184, Fat: 10g, Carbs: 8g, Protein: 6g

Ingredients

→ 1 tablespoon of canola oil

→ 8 pecan mint sprigs

→ ⅓ cup of cream cheese soft

→ 4 peaches

→ 2 tablespoons of honey

Direction

Preheat the grill to med-high heat. Brush the oil on peach halves lightly. Place on the grill & grill for about 5-6 mins. Drizzle a little honey over your peaches & flip them over. In the center of each, put a scoop of cream-cheese-spread. Cook for another 2-3 mins until your filling is heated. Serve with halves of pecan & mint sprigs as a garnish. Serve right away.

PUDDING WITH HONEY BREAD

Prep time: 30mins   **Cook time: 30mins**

Servings: 4

Nutritional information:

Per serving: Kcal 55, Fat: 35g, Carbs: 49g, Protein: 10g

Ingredients

- → 1/4 cup of honey
- → 1 2/3 cup of bread cubes
- → 2 tablespoons of butter
- → 2 eggs
- → chopped walnuts
- → 1/8 teaspoon of salt
- → 1 2/3 cup of hot milk
- → 1/2 teaspoon of vanilla extract

Direction

Preheat your oven to around 350 degrees Fahrenheit. In a baking dish, arrange the cubes of bread. Combine the butter, honey, salt, vanilla essence & eggs in a mixing bowl. Mix thoroughly. While stirring, slowly pour the heated milk in your honey mixture. Slowly pour it over your bread cubes. If preferred, garnish with chopped nuts. Then, put your baking dish into a wider baking dish & bake. Fill the outer dish with water, then bake for around 35 to 40 minutes until your pudding is all set.

Raspberry Brulee

Nutritional information:

Per serving: Kcal 549, Fat: 46g, Carbs: 32g, Protein: 6g

Ingredients	
→ 4 cups whipping cream	→ Raspberries
→ 8 ounces chocolate	→ 8 egg yolks
→ 1/2 cup sugar	→ 2 tablespoons of brown sugar
→ 1 tablespoon of vanilla extract	→ 30 raspberries

Direction

Inside a large mixing bowl, place the chocolate. Bring your cream and half cup of sugar to boil in the large pan. Drizzle over the chocolate and whisk until it is completely smooth. Slowly whisk the mixture of hot cream into the egg yolks, then add the vanilla extract. In each & every of your 10 custard-cups, put 3 raspberries. Divide the custard evenly among the ramekins. Put them in baking-pan and fill with boiling water. Bake for about 40 to 50 minutes at 325°F, uncovered until centers are barely set. Take off the ramekins from the water bath & set aside to cool for approx. 10 mins. Refrigerate them to 4 hours after covering. Combine the leftover sugar with the brown sugar and the remaining sugar and sprinkle this sugar mixture over custards when using a torch for creme-brulee. Using the flame, caramelize the sugar & serve right away.

Rhubarb Crumble

Prep time: 20mins   **Cook time: 60mins**

Servings: 4

Nutritional information:

Per serving: Kcal 440, Fat: 18g, Carbs: 68g, Protein: 4g

Ingredients	
→ 100g sugar	→ 85g butter
→ 500g rhubarb	→ 140g flour
→ 50g walnuts	→ 50g muscovado sugar
→ 3 tbsp of port	

Direction

Place rhubarb pieces in a pan with the port & caster sugar if using. Cook for about 15 minutes, covered, on a low flame, adding extra sugar if desired. Pour your rhubarb onto a baking dish when it is sweet & tender. Preheat the oven to about 200 degrees Celsius. To prepare the topping, you have to rub together cold butter & flour until soft. If using, add chopped walnuts & brown sugar now. Combine the ingredients well. Bake for about 30 minutes, until brown on the top, after scattering the topping on top of rhubarb. Serve with thick-vanilla-custard while it's still hot.

Sherbet With Lime & Cream

Prep time: 20mins   **Cook time: 0mins**

Servings: 4

Nutritional information:

Per serving: Kcal 239, Fat: 7g, Carbs: 41g, Protein: 2g

Ingredients		
→ 1-1/4 cups of sugar	→ 1/3 cup of lime juice
→ 2 cups of whole milk	→ 2 to 3 drops of green food coloring
→ 1 carton whipped topping	→ 1-1/2 teaspoons lime zest

Direction

Combine sugar & milk in a pan. Cook, stirring constantly until the sugar is mixed well & mixture reaches about 175 degrees. Chill for a while. If desired, add the lime zest, juice, and food coloring. Freeze according to the manufacturer's instructions in freezer. Fill a freezer container halfway with sherbet. Allow it soften a little before folding into the whipped topping. Before serving, chill for approx. 4 hours.

Snow Cone With Vanilla Tropical

Prep time: 30mins   **Cook time: 0mins**

Servings: 8

Nutritional information:

Per serving: Kcal 279, Fat: 18g, Carbs: 48g, Protein: 6g

Ingredients		
→ 1 cup of cream	→ 1 teaspoon of vanilla
→ 2 cups of milk	→ 1 can of condensed milk
→ shaved ice	

Direction	
	Combine the cream, milk, condensed milk, & vanilla in a mixing bowl stir well. Place crushed ice in cups or bowls & pour sweet-cream-mixture over each serve. And serve right away.

CHAPTER 6: MEAL PLAN

This chapter has a 7-day sample meal plan as well as 30 days meal plan for you to follow and have a healthy diet if you are going with Intermittent fasting diet patterns. It includes all the recipes you can eat for your breakfast, snacks, lunch and dinner as well.

6.1 7 day Sample Meal Plan (Basic Meal Plan)

Day 1:

- Breakfast: Avocado Quesadillas

- Lunch: Ancient Salmon Burgers

- Snack: Apple Salad With Bok Choy

- Dinner: Asian With Black olives

Day 2:

- Breakfast: Baked Avocado & Eggs With Cheddar Chives
- Lunch: Baked Sardines With Wilted Rocket Salad
- Snack: Detox Thai Tofu Salad
- Dinner: Baked Veggies With Pork

Day 3:

- Breakfast: Berry Parfait
- Lunch: Broccoli With Chicken
- Snack: Amazing Blended Smoothie
- Dinner: Beef Burger

Day 4:

- Breakfast: Blueberry Nut Oatmeal
- Lunch: Chicken & Eggplant
- Snack: Apple Smoothie in Tea
- Dinner: Braised Sauce Lamb With Olives

Day 5:

- Breakfast: Breakfast Butternut Hot Soup
- Lunch: Chicken With Pomegranate Sauce
- Snack: Acorn Squash Stew With Brussels Sprouts
- Dinner: Broccoli With Multiple Veggies

Day 6:

- Breakfast: Divine Apples

- Lunch: Eggplant Steak With Feta Cheese, Black Olives, Roasted Peppers and Chickpeas

- Snack: Baked Eggplants

- Dinner: Citrus Scallops and Shrimp

Day 7:

- Breakfast: Eggs & Bacon With Pecans & Coconut

- Lunch: Grilled Codfish

- Snack: Chia Pudding With Mango, Turmeric and Coconut

- Dinner: Fillets of Broiled Chicken Breasts & Mango

6.2 30 Days Meal Plan

Week 1:

Day 1:

- Breakfast: Avocado Salad with Shrimp/Prawn and Cajun Potato

- Snack: Roasted Beets and Asparagus Salad With Black Cherry Vinaigrette

- Main course: Baked Mahi

Day 2:

- Breakfast: Berries With Butternut Breakfast

- Snack: Fuhrman's Famous Soup

- Main course: Baked Sole

Day 3:

- Breakfast: Black Bean Burrito and Sweet Potato

- Snack: Dip With Cheese & Herbs

- Main course: Brussels Sprouts Creamy Soup

Day 4:

- Breakfast: Bread Pudding With Rhubarb

- Snack: Salad With Cucumber – Dill Cabbage & Lemon Seasoning

- Main course: Chicken Penne Pasta

Day 5:

- Breakfast: Breakfast Shake With Berries

- Snack: Cookies With Meringue

- Main course: Blackened Swordfish

Day 6:

- Breakfast: Egg Plant in Slow Cooker

- Snack: Crunchy Sweet Potato Stew

- Main course: Broccoli dal Curry

Day 7:

- Breakfast: Fast Banana Berries Breakfast

- Snack: Salad With Strawberry & Watercress With Almond Seasoning

- Main course: Brussel Sprout and Sheet Pan Chicken

Day 8:

- Breakfast: Fruity Breakfast Salad

- Snack: Qu Kale Soup

- Main course: Crockpot Black-Eyed Peas

Week 2:

Day 1:

- Breakfast: Mum's Supper Club le Parmesan

- Snack: Berry Banana Smoothie

- Main course: Curry Salmon With Black Cabbage

Day 2:

- Breakfast: Omelet With Cheddar citru & Mushrooms

- Snack: Pomegranate Refresher

- Main course: Greek Chicken & Beans

Day 3:

- Breakfast: Pancakes With Blueberry & Almond

- Snack: Three Bean Mango Salad

- Main course: Grilled Garlic Lamb Chops

Day 4:

- Breakfast: Pudding With Corn

- Snack: Snow Cone With Vanilla Tropical

- Main course: Grilled Tuna

Day 5:

- Breakfast: Sausages & Almond Milk

- Snack: Sherbet With Lime & Cream

- Main course: Fish With Olives, Tomatoes and Capers

Day 6:

- Breakfast: Scrambled Tuscan Tofu

- Snack: Pudding With Honey Bread

- Main course: Green Olives With Lemon Mutton

Day 7:

- Breakfast: Baked Avocado & Eggs With Cheddar Chives

- Snack: Pavlova With Peaches

- Main course: Lamb & Coconut

Day 8:

- Breakfast: Frittata di Polenta

- Snack: Antioxidant Power Juice

- Main course: Linguine and Mixed Seafood

Week 3:

Day 1:

- Snack: Quick Homemade Tomato Gazpacho

- Main course: Liver With avocado & Shallots

Day 2:

- Snack: Salad With Ginger Beef

- Main course: Oatmeal With Pecans & Coconut

Day 3:

- Snack: Apple Smoothie With Oatberries

- Main course: Old Lamb Granny Burger

Day 4:

- Snack: Granita D'apple Tart

- Main course: Pasta & Shrimps

Day 5:

- Snack: Couscous Pudding With Vanilla

- Main course: Pork Chops With Sage

Day 6:

- Snack: Tortilla Chips With Cinnamon

- Main course: Poached Eggs and Avocado Toast

Day 7:

- Snack: Boston Emerald Smoothie
- Main course: Mediterranean Chicken Breast With Avocado Tapenade

Week 4:

Day 1:

- Snack: Ice Milk With Candied Ginger
- Main course: Quick Halibust Dish

Day 2:

- Snack: Corn With grilled & Spicy Kettle
- Main course: Seared Calf's Liver

Day 3:

- Snack: Chicken Crostini With Roasted Red Pepper
- Main course: Mushrooms and Olives Braised Pork

Day 4:

- Snack: Detoxifying Green Tea
- Main course: Quinoa Breakfast Pudding

Day 5:

- Snack: Baked garlic Dip

- Main course: Spicy Rigatoni With Mussels

Day 6:

- Snack: Black Forest Soup With Mushrooms in Cream

- Main course: Stuffed Sesame Chicken Breasts

Day 7:

- Snack: Smoothie of Watermelon & Raspberries

- Main course: Fast Banana Berries Breakfast

Chapter 7: First month of Intermittent Fasting

This chapter gives detail about the changes you have to expect during Intermittent fasting. How 1st month of your IF will go, how you can achieve goals with healthy progress & how to enjoy this eating-fasting diet pattern is also discussed in detail and depth.

7.1 Changes you can expect

It takes time

It's only normal to want to see results as quickly as possible after putting in the effort. To go right past the awkward rookie stage and into the comfortable seasoned pro stage, or at the very least to the level where you can claim you kind of know what you are doing, is to be successful. To pass through this first stage of learning, on the other hand, is to set oneself up for failure. It's important to give your body ample time to adjust to fasting, particularly if this is your first time doing so.

You will be better prepared to cope with any difficulties that may arise due to going through this procedure. Never lose faith in the process and never give up even when things become difficult; remember that no one is perfect the first time they try anything. You will eventually adapt and take the first step toward acquiring the mentality you will need to succeed if you continue on your current path.

Weight loss

Many people who experiment with intermittent fasting do it in order to reduce weight. In general, intermittent fasting causes you to consume fewer meals. You'll consume less calories though you adjust by eating substantially more at the other meals. Intermittent fasting also improves hormone function, which aids in weight reduction.

Lower levels of insulin, greater levels of HGH, and enhanced norepinephrine levels all help the body burn down fat & utilize it for energy. As a result, short-period fasting boosts your metabolism, allowing you to consume far more calories. Intermittent fasting, in other words, works on the both ends of the caloric equation. It raises your metabolism (calories burned) while decreasing the quantity of food you consume (reduces intake of calories).

More energy

It takes a lot of energy and effort to start something new & tricky. If nothing else is working for you, intermittent fasting may be the solution. However, it is neither a quick fix nor a shortcut to achieving your goals. It is just another nutritional arrangement that may be quite helpful for some persons when used appropriately and in conjunction with a person's lifestyle. If you fast, you must keep this in mind and remember that the consequences are reliant on you, even if they are spectacular in their effects.

- Remaining committed to a regular training program.

- Employing approaches for gradual overloading.

- Achieving your daily calorie and macronutrient goals is important.

Whether they are based on intermittent fasting or something else, all diet configurations must consider the factors mentioned above.

Maintaining a social life

You'll most likely be out with pals late at night. You may change your fasting & eating period for the day and resume your routine the next day. You must plan your outings with friends within your eating window. This will help you stick to the intermittent fasting strategy and meet your fitness and weight reduction objectives.

Note that you can consume anything you want within your eating periods by doing intermittent fasting. Bring some fasting goods with you so that you may continue to enjoy yourself with your friends even if the fun lasts longer than your eating time. This might not be easy since your social life is usually centered on food and beverages. You may, however, be inventive and come up with new methods to connect with your pals that do not involve eating or drinking. You'll be able to concentrate more on intermittent fasting this way.

Better sleep

Intermittent fasting may enhance the quality of sleep by strengthening your circadian rhythms. Circadian rhythms control various biological systems, including hunger, metabolism, and sleep-wake cycles, and the primary circadian is sunlight. Still, the food is a potent supplementary time cue; following a defined meal schedule, such as fasting, may reinforce your natural circadian rhythms.

Intermittent fasters had more significant amounts of growth hormone than non-intermittent fasters. This hormone, formed during sleep, consumes fat, repairs muscles, and aids in cellular regeneration. Therefore, those who fast may feel more energized and replenished when they wake up. Intermittent fasting participants may also feel an increase in energy and attention. Fasting boosts orexin, which is linked to alertness.

Fasters had lower orexin-A amounts at night and greater levels during the day, making them feel more awake and sleep more soundly.

Enjoying a routine

If correctly performed, intermittent fasting may result in considerable benefits in terms of dietary freedom and, consequently, in terms of the enjoyment of one's diet when done correctly. The reason for this is that skipping breakfast may save you calories each day, depending on what you generally eat first thing in the morning. Change the calories in your diet from your breakfast to your lunch, dinner, and one or two snacks to make your diet more pleasurable.

How about if you are attending a friend's birthday dinner at a restaurant later in the evening? It's not a problem at all. Rather than skipping breakfast, opt for a protein-packed lunch to guarantee that you have enough calories to enjoy the evening without exceeding your daily calorie consumption restriction.

CHAPTER 8: EXERCISE SUGGESTION FOR WOMEN OVER 50

This chapter gives detail about the right exercise recommendations for aging women. How much exercise should you usually get, what are the basic types of exercises & benefits for women over 50 are also discussed in detail and depth.

8.1 How much exercise should you get?

Although we've long known about the advantages of exercise as a proactive strategy to improve our physical health and fight illness, exercise is also being acknowledged as a crucial component in achieving and maintaining mental fitness. So, if you currently engage in some physical activity, pat yourself on the back since you are increasing both your physical and mental health.

The quantity of exercise that is advised for women over 50 age limit is as similar as for other individuals. Each week, try to get in for about 150 mins of moderate or 75 mins of strenuous exercise at least. This equates to half hour of moderate activity or 15 mins of intensive exercise 5 days per week. This is also a great idea to do balancing exercises minimum 3 times a week if you have restricted mobility and are at danger of falling.

Brisk Walking

Aerobic exercise of moderate intensity involves an example of brisk walking. Anything that causes a person to sweat and boosts their rate of heart to the point where they are only able to speak but can't sing. A person may be considered brisk walking if they walk at a maximum pace of 4.5 miles per hour according to thumb rule. Every day, for about 30 mins, an individual should go for a vigorous walk.

Pool Workouts

Water exercises are a great approach to improve your fitness cardio also while strengthening your primary muscle groups. Anyone with joint problems or injuries, and those who are expecting or have balance challenges, can benefit from pool workouts. Warmer water enhances joint mobility and offers a low-impact environment for movements. There are various types of effective pool workouts. These exercises may help you feel better about your regular mobility.

Weight-Bearing Exercises

After the age of 30, bone mass begins to deteriorate. Resistance training protects loads bones & skeletal muscle, eventually encouraging cells forming bones, and studies have found that this sort of activity is helpful in maintaining bone mineral density in postmenopausal women. Any weight-bearing exercise that has any influence on the bones can improve bone health. Hiking, practicing sports like dancing or tennis are all excellent methods to receive bonuses for bone mass maintenance.

Resistance Training

Sarcopenia is a muscular loss and weakening condition that affects the elderly. It's time for the opportunity to work out in a method that will help you retain the mass of muscle that will further keep you flexible and functional as you age. Weights should be picked up. Resistance exercise is really an effective technique to combat this problem since it challenges and develops muscles. Throughout the whole body, major muscle groups are targeted. Using functional moves that mirror how the body moves on a daily basis. A deadlift, for example, is a resistance workout that may help you pick things up.

Biking

The combo of being outside and moving your body is excellent for your cognitive powers. According to a research involving

100 persons aged 50 and older who were divided into 3 groups: a group with cycling, a group with e-bikes, or the last one was control group who did not drive at all. For 8 weeks, those allocated to the e-bike or cycling group were told to ride their bikes for about half hour 3 times a week. Biking, whether on an e-bike or a pedal cycle, improved executive function & well-being in participants.

Yoga

Approximately 40% of yoga practitioners in the US are above the age of fifty. Some women over the age of 50 have been doing yoga for years, if not decades, while others are discovering it for the first time in their 50s. When it comes to yoga, it's crucial to recognize that there are many various sorts of styles to choose from. Some kinds of yoga, regardless of age, maybe excessively fast-paced, hard, or physically demanding for some persons, while other styles are intended to be therapeutic and soothing. You should generally adhere to softer kinds of yoga unless you are experienced. These types of yoga are more focused on stretching and balancing than on increasing strength and muscle.

It is recommended that you attempt chair yoga since it is one of the finest methods to start yoga and begin a fitness program if you haven't been physically active in the past. It is a kind of yoga in which you execute several positions while sitting on a chair or standing with the assistance of a chair.

Exercising while Fasting

It is totally fine to exercise while fasting for hormone optimization, not only calories & workout, is the secret to weight reduction and muscle building. Intermittent fasting has been shown to have incredible advantages on its own, but joining it with training known as sprint training raises the benefits of both to an entire new level. When you combine the two, you'll have more growth hormone & be more prone to insulin, which is crucial for keeping young and slender.

Many individuals stress about calories in vs. calories out and are concerned about muscle loss, which may occur if you workout without refueling. When you realize how advantageous exercising, while fasted, has on the body's hormones, you'll discover that fasting & workout are not just fine, but they're the best approach to improve your body composition as well as health.

Benefits of exercise for women over 50

Being physically active enhance years of the life and provides plenty of other advantages as well, such as:

- Maintains or loses weight

- Helps to combat slight illness as well as chronic disease

- Decreased Inflammation

- Supports mobility, flexibility, and balance.

- Helps with mental health

CHAPTER 9: MISTAKES TO AVOID

This chapter gives detail about the mistakes you should avoid during Intermittent fasting. You should be aware of all these tricky situations, and how to handle them is also discussed in detail and depth.

Off to a drastic start

The worst blunder you can make is to start out too quickly. You should be quite up for disappointment if you plunge into IF without first going easy into it. It might be difficult to transition from eating three appropriate meals or six little meals in a day to taking your foods within a window of 4-hour, for instance. Instead, gradually introduce fasting.

Selecting the wrong Intermittent fasting plan

You're ready to attempt intermittent fasting for weight reduction, and you've stocked your pantry with whole meals such as fish and poultry, fruits and vegetables, and nutritious sides like quinoa and lentils to get you started. The issue is that you haven't picked a proper strategy that will put you in the best position to succeed. Rather than rushing into a plan without giving it much thought, take some time to examine your lifestyle and determine which plan would work best for your schedule and habits.

Consuming wrong foods during the eating window

The error of eating the incorrect things when fasting goes hand in hand with the problem of overeating. If you have an 8-hour fasting window and fill it with processed, greasy, or sugary meals, you are not going to feel good at all, according to the experts.

Be sure to eat healthy whole foods. Proteins, good fats, walnuts, lentils, unprocessed grains, and whole vegetables and fruits comprise the foundation of your nutritional plan.

- Keep an eye on your salt consumption, and be on the lookout for hidden sweets.

- Instead of packaged meals, prepare real foods to save money.

- Fill half of your plate with fiber, nutritious carbohydrates and fats, and lean proteins to round off your meal.

Severe calorie restriction during the eating window

There exists such a thing as decreasing your calorie intake too much. It is not recommended to consume fewer than 1200 calories during your fasting window. Not only that, but it may also have a negative impact on your metabolism. If you slow your digestion down too much, you will start to lose lean muscle rather than gain it, which is counterproductive.

To avoid making this error, consider planning your meals for the next week on the weekend. This provides you with balanced, healthful meals that are ready to eat at your convenience. When it comes time to dine, you may look forward to a wholesome, nutritional, and caloric-correct meal.

Not keeping your body hydrated

Maintaining proper hydration is critical during intermittent fasting. Keep in mind that your body is not absorbing the water that would normally be taken with meals. As a result, if you are not cautious, adverse effects might lead you to lose your balance. If you let yourself get dehydrated, you may experience:

- Headaches

- Muscular cramps

- Acute hunger pangs

Unknowingly breaking fast

It's important to be mindful of hidden breakers of fast. You should know that actually, the flavor of sweetness makes your brain release insulin. This triggers the release of insulin, thereby breaking the fast. Breaking the fast is a very common

IF Intermittent Fasting blunder. When you're not eating, clean your teeth with a paste of water & baking soda. Also, read the instructions carefully prior taking supplements & vitamins.

Not forgiving yourself

One mistake does not equal to failure. You'll have times when an Intermittent Fasting diet is especially difficult, and you don't think that you'll be able to keep up. It's pretty fine to take a short break if necessary. Set aside a day to concentrate. Stick to your healthy plan for eating, but indulge in treats like a serving of delicious, healthy beef with broccoli or a wonderful protein smoothie the next day.

Not exercising regularly

Some individuals believe that they cannot exercise during a fasting phase when this is the optimum situation in reality. Exercise aids in the burning of fat that has been accumulated. Additionally, while you exercise, the growth hormone levels rise, which aids in the development of lean muscle mass. However, there are certain guidelines to follow to get the most out of your exercises.

Keep the following factors in mind to get the greatest outcomes from your efforts:

- Workouts should be scheduled within meal hours, and healthy carbohydrates and proteins should be consumed within 30 minutes after the activity.

- If the activity is strenuous, make sure you eat beforehand so that your glycogen reserves are fully replenished after the workout.

- Exercise should be tailored to the fasting approach; for example, if you are fasting for 24 hours, you should avoid engaging in strenuous activity on that day.

- Maintaining enough hydration during the fast, and particularly during the exercise, is essential.

- Pay attention to your body's signals; if you begin to feel dizzy or lightheaded, take a break or stop the exercise immediately.

CHAPTER 10: HEALTHY DIET TIPS AND SUGGESTIONS

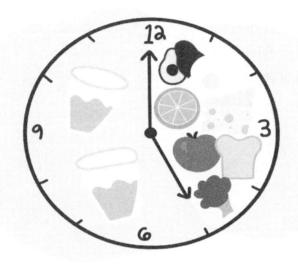

This chapter gives detail about the healthy diet tips and suggestions for doing Intermittent fasting. How to follow them is also included in the chapter with depth & detail.

10.1 Tips & suggestions

Best food choices while following Intermittent fasting

Pick healthy foods for your meals during IF. Meals that are rich in nutrients should be preferred.

Start your day with water

Keep yourself hydrated while following Intermittent fasting.

Pick the right drink

Use appropriate liquids during your IF routine.

Reduce sugar consumption

Try to decrease your sugar consumption and follow as suggested in your meal plan.

Avoid oily foods

Avoid consuming oily foods while following Intermittent fasting. Instead, go and opt for healthy food options which are rich in nutrients.

Strength training helps

Strength training exercises will help you to boost your energy during IF.

Pay attention to Sodium intake

You have to be careful and get yourself aware of the Sodium intake that your body demands so that you can satisfy the required intake.

Increase Calcium intake

Increase your Calcium intake during Intermittent fasting.

Preventive screenings

Make accountability after a few days to check whether you are going right with the plan or not.

Get sufficient sleep

Try to have enough sleep so that you can feel motivated and full of energy to restart your day and IF routine.

Eat healthily

Consume healthy foods in your eating window and design your meal plans accordingly.

Maintain a food journal

Keep your food journal up-to-date as it will help you to remind your mandatory meal proportions.

Know your BMI and how to calculate it

Learn about your Body Mass Index that what it is, and also know the formula that how you can calculate it whenever needed. It helps you to be aware of your progress while following IF.

Check progress

You have to check after regular intervals that either you are progressing rightly during both of your eating as well as fasting windows, or there is a need for some improvement.

Do your homework

Try to follow your short-term goals with consistency so that you can easily achieve long-term goals.

Visualization

Visualization is basically to change intentionally how you feel, think & approach various scenarios of your life. Master the trick of seeing with the deep vision to know the rights or wrongs of your practices; that is how one can progress more quickly towards the major goal.

Support system

Stay connected with your support system to enhance your productivity, to keep yourself motivated and to achieve the best results.

Keep yourself distracted during fasts

Fasting is such a challenging task so keep yourself involved in some productive activities. In this way, one can easily manage his/her fasting hours and stay in mental balance as well because you got distracted in a healthy manner.

Manage the stress

Stress is an unavoidable aspect of everyday living. No matter how much we would want for a stress-free life, the truth is that stress is required for survival. It may have a detrimental impact on our lives depending on how we react to it. Learning to manage stress appropriately may benefit both our physical and mental health. Techniques such as meditation and other relaxation methods, exercise, and visualization may all be beneficial in minimizing the detrimental effects of stress on the body.

COOKING CONVERSION CHART

Measurement

CUP	ONCES	MILLILITERS	TABLESPOONS
8 cup	64 oz	1895 ml	128
6 cup	48 oz	1420 ml	96
5 cup	40 oz	1180 ml	80
4 cup	32 oz	960 ml	64
2 cup	16 oz	480 ml	32
1 cup	8 oz	240 ml	16
3/4 cup	6 oz	177 ml	12
2/3 cup	5 oz	158 ml	11
1/2 cup	4 oz	118 ml	8
3/8 cup	3 oz	90 ml	6
1/3 cup	2.5 oz	79 ml	5.5
1/4 cup	2 oz	59 ml	4
1/8 cup	1 oz	30 ml	3
1/16 cup	1/2 oz	15 ml	1

Temperature

FAHRENHEIT	CELSIUS
100 °F	37 °C
150 °F	65 °C
200 °F	93 °C
250 °F	121 °C
300 °F	150 °C
325 °F	160 °C
350 °F	180 °C
375 °F	190 °C
400 °F	200 °C
425 °F	220 °C
450 °F	230 °C
500 °F	260 °C
525 °F	274 °C
550 °F	288 °C

Weight

IMPERIAL	METRIC
1/2 oz	15 g
1 oz	29 g
2 oz	57 g
3 oz	85 g
4 oz	113 g
5 oz	141 g
6 oz	170 g
8 oz	227 g
10 oz	283 g
12 oz	340 g
13 oz	369 g
14 oz	397 g
15 oz	425 g
1 lb	453 g

CONCLUSION

The Intermittent fasting diet does not need you to keep track of your calories or macronutrient intake, contrasting with most other diets. There are no limitations on the foods that may be taken or avoided. Therefore it is more of a lifestyle decision than a diet in this case. To reduce weight, many people turn to intermittent fasting, which is a simple, practical, and effective strategy of eating less while simultaneously decreasing weight and lowering body fat percentage. This supplement may also help avoid heart disease and diabetes, maintain muscle mass, and enhance overall psychological well-being. As a bonus, since there will be fewer meals to plan, prepare and cook, this eating pattern may allow you to save time in the kitchen and money. When it comes to dieting, no one approach or plan works for everyone. This holds for people who engage in intermittent fasting as well as for the general public. When it comes to fasting, women should approach it less tense than men should, across the whole spectrum. For example, shorter fasting periods, certain fasting days, and consuming a minimal number of calories on the fasting days may be necessary to attain this goal.

Regardless of your approach, it is still crucial to keep a nutritious diet when you are not fasting. Consider the following scenario: you eat a substantial amount of unhealthy, calorie meals during non-fasting hours. If this is the case, probably, you may not experience the same weight loss and health benefits as you would normally. The most successful technique is to endure and sustain without suffering any negative health consequences for an extended period. It is permissible to fast intermittently as often or as seldom as required to satisfy your nutritional needs. Many people mix and match strategies throughout the year, practicing some daily and others monthly or yearly for optimum results. All approaches are useful, but only through research, trial, and error will you be able to identify which one is the most helpful for you in your particular situation. Before commencing a fasting program, you must check with your doctor first.

Printed in Great Britain
by Amazon